Aquaponics for Beginners

How to Build your own Aquaponic Garden that will Grow Organic Vegetables

Table of Contents

About me

I love aquaponics. This book is a collection of my notes throughout the years of researching different types of aquaponic systems. I have made sure to include everything you need to know to get started with aquaponics.

I hope you find this book useful and start your aquaponics journey using the knowledge shared in this book. Lend this book to your friends so they can begin their journey!

I'm the owner of howtoaquaponic.com, where I share the latest tips and techniques about aquaponic gardening. If you finish this book, you can become a fan of the Facebook group where you can ask questions and show off your system.

- https://www.facebook.com/groups/howtoaquaponic
- https://www.howtoaquaponic.com

Let's get started!

Introduction to Aquaponics

Aquaponics is simply the combination of fish and plants. Perhaps calling it "Fish & Plants in Harmony" could be a good name, but it doesn't have quite the same ring to it than aquaponics does.

You need to keep the fish in a dedicated area. The water containing their waste products are processed by a biological filter and then directed to your plants.

This provides your plants with most of the nutrients they need. A perfectly run aquaponics system needs fish food and three additional nutrients that the fish or fish food can't provide. The reward is fish and accelerated plant growth.

Fish $\longrightarrow$ Nutrients $\longrightarrow$ Plants

OR

Fish feed $\longrightarrow$ Ammonia $\longrightarrow$ Nitrites $\longrightarrow$ Nitrates $\longrightarrow$ Plant growth

Aquaponics is not a new discovery. The Aztecs were known to have created a system of islands with canals. Each island was dedicated to plant growth with the aid of the canal water and the mud, which was full of nutrients. This made the ideal growing media for the plants, which flourished. That was 1,000 AD!

Aquaponics in its early stages

The paddy fields in Asia are a great example of hydroculture in ancient times. Many Asian farmers still use the flood and drain technique today. Some ancient Chinese even took it one step further and utilized catfish, finfish, and plants together.

Why Aquaponics?

Aquaponics is enjoying a resurgence in popularity across the world. The simple reason for this is the current number of people in the world and the lack of (organic) food.

An aquaponics system can produce fish and plants to eat while taking up considerably less space than traditional farming methods.

The problem is that until recently, fish breeding and farming were undertaken in coastal areas using nets to close off individual sections.

Inland lakes have also been used or created for the same purpose. A refined version of this is known as re-circulating aquaculture systems or simply RAS., this allows the farmers to stock the water with a much larger quantity of fish than the traditional netted off areas.

Netted aquaculture fish farm in a lake

Unfortunately, a large amount of antibiotics is needed to keep the fish healthy, and there is a significant amount of waste produced. Both increase the cost of this type of breeding and potentially damages the environment for other living animals and humans.

Aquaponics offers a more environmentally friendly way of breeding fish, with the added benefit of accelerated plant growth.

Hydroponics is also a method of growing plants. In this type of system, the plants have their roots exposed to a nutrient-rich solution that is dissolved in the water.

These nutrients generally come from chemical products. This is used to create a solution that runs under the plants, inciting growth while reducing the risk of disease and pests.

Hydroponics is effective, but in many cases, it requires chemicals. The water in a hydroponics system must be partially dumped and replaced.

In contrast, aquaponics systems are almost entirely self-contained. The water generally doesn't need to be replaced, while the density of fish and plants can be impressively high.

Despite the long history of aquaponics, the first large scale example of productive utilization in the modern world dates from the mid-1980s.

Aquaponics is not just better for productivity and reducing environmental issues. It is also an effective method of growing organic plants without using large amounts of water. A properly closed-loop aquaponics system will need 10% of the water soil growing does.

It is worth noting that there are several critical differences between aquaponics and hydroponics:

Time to Start-Up
Hydroponic systems need a reservoir for you to fill with the nutrient-rich solution. Then, you're ready to put your growing media in and get started. This is much faster than an aquaponics system, which can take up to 6 weeks for the bacteria to colonize the system.

Bacteria
Hydroponics systems rely on a sterile environment, while aquaponics needs nitrifying bacteria to complete the process of converting fish food to available nutrients.

Productivity
Research from MDPI (Basel, Switzerland) shows that aquaponics systems are similar or at least equal to growing hydroponically in an NFT setup.

Read the study here:
https://www.howtoaquaponic.com/basel-research

Maintenance
A well designed and run aquaponics system needs very little maintenance. All the elements should balance naturally, making the system self-contained. Other than planting and harvesting, you will need to:

- Check for pH, ammonia, nitrites, and temperature
- Remove solids from the filter
- Check for pests
- Feed the fish (can be automated)

Simplicity
An aquaponics system can be more complicated to design than a hydroponics system. Although nutrient mixing can become quite complicated in hydroponics as well.

Each system has its pros and cons, but who doesn't like to grow plants with the added benefit of fish?

Nutrient Cycle

The nutrient cycle of aquaponics can be quite overwhelming. I will explain it using the following graphic:

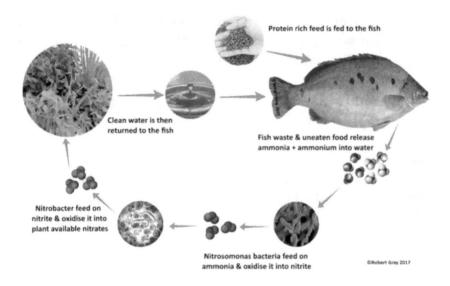

Protein rich feed is fed to the fish

Clean water is then returned to the fish

Fish waste & uneaten food release ammonia + ammonium into water

Nitrobacter feed on nitrite & oxidise it into plant available nitrates

Nitrosomonas bacteria feed on ammonia & oxidise it into nitrite

©Robert Gray 2017

Thanks to Robert Gray for providing this graphic

1. The fish break down the fish feed to toxic ammonia and the less toxic ammonium. Fish also create ammonia and ammonium through their gills.

2. If there is no bacteria to break down the ammonia and ammonium, your fish will die. That's why we need bacteria in our system. The bacteria love oxygenated water, and they will colonize the entire surface area of your system. The surface area will be:

    A. Your grow beds or biofilter
    B. The surface area of your pipes, and fish tank

3. It takes some time for bacteria to populate the surface area of your system. But when they do, the Nitrosomonas bacteria convert the toxic ammonia to nitrites. But nitrites are still toxic to the system.

4. Other bacteria in the system called Nitrobacter will convert the nitrites to nitrates.

5. Plants love nitrates, and they will take the nutrients out of the water before returning it to the fish tank. Then the cycle repeats itself.

This is a very simplified way of explaining how aquaponics works. I will gradually increase the information throughout this book so you won't become overwhelmed.

Types of Aquaponic Systems

Most of the time, you will only see one type of aquaponics system in people's DIY setups, and that is the media filled bed. There are some other systems we are going to look at here.
We will cover the most popular one first for the backyard gardener.

The Media Filled Bed

This is generally considered the easiest form of aquaponics and the best one for beginners to start with. Why? Because it acts as grow media and a bio-filter in one. The media filled bed is also called a grow bed.

A grow bed is mainly used as a place to house the nitrifying bacteria. The bed will also be used as a growing/securing media for the plants.

Generally, grow beds are used with larger plants that need big roots to keep them upright. Because the recommended depth of these beds is 12 inches deep, they are perfect for growing tomato plants or even fruiting trees.

Pros
- Great variety to grow crops.
- It doesn't need extra filtration (if using the right ratio).
- Constant mineralization (if worms are added).
- Good learning experience for beginners.
- It can be combined with commercial operations to reduce suspended solids.

Cons

- The most expensive system for the available grow area.
- Labor intensive.
- Not efficient for bigger installations.

Continuous or flood and drain

There are two types of systems for the media bed. The first one is called continuous flow, while the other is known as flood and drain or ebb and flow.

Continuous flow

This system will keep your grow beds filled at a constant level. This means the media will be submerged all the time without letting oxygen access the roots. This could be problematic if you don't have enough aeration in your system. The bacteria need oxygen to thrive. That's why I don't recommend using a continuous flow system.

It doesn't guarantee seamless operation, and I would be checking my water for its oxygen level all the time.

Flood and drain

Instead, I suggest using the flood and drain method as it gives peace of mind, and you don't have to monitor oxygen levels that often.

The flood and drain cycle will use a siphon method to let the whole media bed fill with water and then drain again using a siphon. This way, the growing media, and the roots will be exposed to the air in every cycle. This promotes bacteria to grow and the roots to be exposed to oxygen.

The Siphon

So how is the water drained, you might ask?

We use something called a siphon. There are two main types of siphons. I'm going to explain the easy version first and then the more popular and complex bell siphon.

Option 1 - Timer
With this siphon, you need a timer for your pump. This way, your system requires less energy while still doing the same as the bell siphon. This method is preferred for beginners.

In this image, you can see the water from the fish tank being pumped up to the grow beds. Here, the water level is at its highest. The excess water will be drained by the 'open pipe for overflow.'

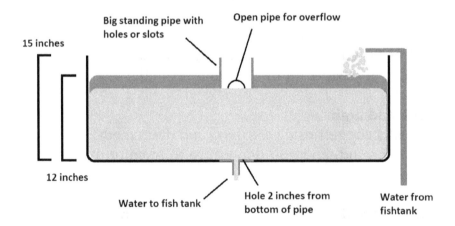

There are little slots drilled or cut in the middle of the big standing pipe. This allows the water to flow to the middle of the big standing pipe. The slots in the big standing pipe need to be small enough to not to let grow media (rocks) to get through.

There is a smaller standing pipe inside the big standing pipe that's directly connected to your fish tank with a bulkhead fitting or uniseal. This pipe will allow the water to flow back to the fish tank and act as an overflow. Remember that the diameter of the small standing pipe must be big enough in order to function as an overflow (at least one inch).

1. The timer initiates, and the pump moves the water from the fish tank up to the growbed. The growbed starts to fill with water.

2. The water level in the growbed rises to the level of the overflow (the small standing pipe). The excess water that gets pumped in the growbed will exit the overflow back to the fish tank. Let it overflow for a few minutes.

3. The timer will stop, and the pump will shut down. The water will slowly drain through the small hole at the bottom of the small standing pipe.

4. After the growbed has fully drained, the timer initiates again, and the growbed will start to fill up again, repeating the cycle.

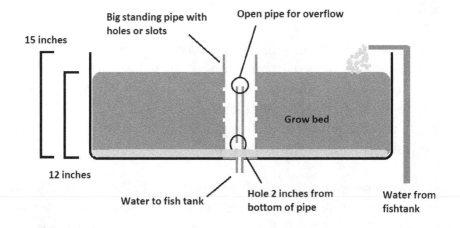

Big standing pipe with holes or slots

Open pipe for overflow

15 inches

12 inches

Grow bed

Water to fish tank

Hole 2 inches from bottom of pipe

Water from fishtank

Because every growbed is different in size, you need to watch how long it takes for your growbed to drain and fill up fully. Then, adjust your timer.

Note:
While the bed is filling up, the water will drain from the small hole in the standing pipe. But the hole at the bottom of the standing pipe will be quite small. You need to make sure that the flow rate of the small hole is less than the flow rate of the water that is being pumped in your grow bed.

The size of this hole is crucial, drill it too small, and your grow bed will drain slowly. Drill it too big and the grow bed will fill up very slowly.

Option 2: Bell Siphon
The bell siphon is a great way to manage a flood and drain cycle naturally. We've already looked at its basic function: to help flood and drain the growbed. But let's look at it in a little more detail.

It is always a good idea to have an overflow pipe feeding back to the tank; this will prevent the water from overflowing your grow beds if you have a problem with the drainage through the bell siphon.

The basic bell siphon will simply have a ¾ inch (19mm) pipe running up to approximately one inch below the top of the growing media. You will then have a bigger inverted pipe (dome) over the pipe, which sticks just out of the water. There needs to be a gap at the bottom of the inverted pipe to ensure the water can get to the drain pipe.

The drain pipe you have just installed will be full of air. As the water moves up in your tank, it will eventually reach the top of the pipe. This will block the air and cause a vacuum in the pipe.

The vacuum will then suck the water down the pipe and keep moving water until the level is below the top of the pipe.
At this point, the pipe draws in air instead of water and stops draining the water from your grow bed to your fish tank. This is what we call: 'the siphon breaks.'

After the siphon breaks, the growbed will fill up again.

Top view of the bell siphon (image from aquaponicsexposed.com)

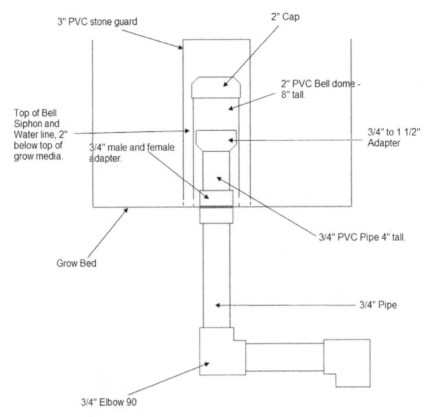

A bell siphon in detail. Thanks to Spaceman Spiff for the image

There are two key points that need to be addressed: getting the siphon to start with a lower water flow and giving it a good flow rate.

It is possible to reduce the siphon starting point by adding a pinch in your exit pipe. However, this will also reduce the flow rate of your water, which is not desirable.

Instead of a pinch, you could add a 90-degree elbow into your system just below the tank. This would create a turbulence spot which would improve the efficiency of air movement and lower the amount of water needed to start the siphon. However, this will also reduce the equilibrium flow and not aid your ability to create a reliable siphon effect.

The best solution is to increase the size of the pipe for the last inch or two as it reaches the top of your grow bed (¾ to 1½ adapter). This simple adjustment will turn the main pipe into a pinch effect without reducing the flow rate. In short, you'll get a low flow in the beginning, and it increases in power once the siphon has initiated.

The speed of water removal will ensure the siphon breaks, and the flood and drain part of your system remains working efficiently.

This simple technique works as the larger area at the top of the siphon pipe creates a strong starting flow combined with the reducing width of the pipe and, if possible, a longer pipe outside of your tank. This will reduce the amount of water you need to start your siphon effect.

The equilibrium flow will be stopped by the continual residual flow and the funnel at the top of your pipe, causing a water imbalance that will shut down the siphoning effect.

Tips to Get Your System Draining Properly
Now that you know how to make your own siphon, the following tips will help you to ensure it is working properly:

- The pipe in your grow bed must be level. If it is leaning, then you will change the flow rate of your drain, which is likely to change the equilibrium flow.

- It is best to put your bell siphon at either the center of your tank or at the furthest possible point from the entry of water to your tank.

- Blockages can still occur in your siphon. It is essential to check the pipes regularly for root-bound crops.

The greatest advantage of creating and installing a bell siphon into your aquaponics system is that once you've got it set up, it will keep working without you needing to interfere or be present. If you are running a bell siphon system, you don't need to use a timer for the pump. The pump will run continuously. The flow rate of the suction created by the siphon will be greater than the water coming in.

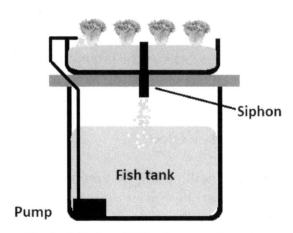

Typical Cut and Flip Aquaponics setup

Funnel   **Bell**   **Stone guard**

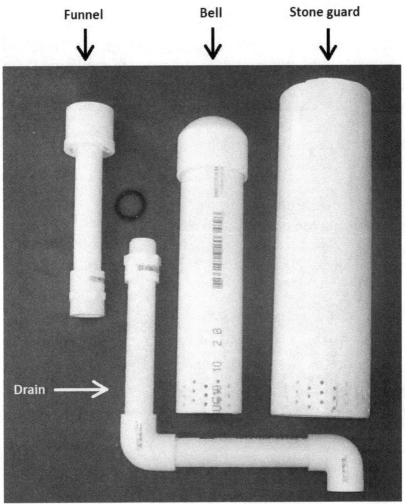

Thanks to Spaceman Spiff for the image

Aim for your entire fish tank to cycle through your system in one to two hours.

Do not oversize your pump if you are not using a split flow from a sump tank. Oversizing your pump could make the tuning of your bell siphon difficult. Too much flow means longer cycle times and potentially flooding the growbed.

We go more in-depth on the size of the pump you need later.

Types of Media

The final stage in understanding the media beds is acknowledging the different types of growing media that you can use. The growing media will be placed in your grow bed. It is there to house the bacteria and to hold your plants in place.

When you are deciding on which media to use, you are looking for these two factors:

- High surface area.
- Avoiding the possibility to clog up.

Expanded Clay or Hydroton

These are balls of clay that have been heated to extremely high temperatures. This makes them very light but extremely porous, making it a good media for bacteria.

The fact that they have been baked also means they won't degrade; they are pH neutral, and they are easy to handle. They don't cut your hands like other media does.

Expanded Shale

This is crushed before it is heated to high temperatures. The effect is the same as with the clay pebbles. It is clean, porous, and pH neutral. Expanded shale is also very light and has a large surface area, making it very effective to house bacteria.

Lava Rock

Lava rock is surprisingly light and extremely porous. It has been used as a growing medium for many years. The nature of this rock ensures excellent surface area. They are also pH neutral.

They are also used in garden ponds to house bacteria. Making it easy to source them from a pond store nearby.

They are generally very sharp, which means they can cut your hands and even damage the root of the plants if you move the rocks.

River Rock

River rock is a very good and cheap alternative to expanded clay. The only downside to it is its weight. If you are on a budget, river rock is the perfect choice for you. It's easy on the hands and available literally everywhere. I recommend using ¾ inch river rock.

Gravel

This is a great option if you are on a tight budget as it tends to be the cheapest and easiest grow media to get. But it can give you a few problems.

Gravel tends to bunch together exceptionally well. This makes it a dense material for a plant to find its way through. While this shouldn't be an issue if you have tall plants with long roots, it will be a problem for most of the smaller plants.

If you do use gravel, you should always wash them first and do a vinegar test before putting it in your tank. It is possible that there will be limestone in it, which will increase the pH of the water.

How to do a vinegar test:
Take a handful of your washed gravel and put it in a cup (preferably transparent). Then fill it up with white vinegar. If you see it fizzing (like soda), you have limestone in it. If you see signs of limestone, you shouldn't use it. Test a few batches of it before deciding. Do not use it if you see signs of limestone.

It may seem like a lot to take in, but once you understand the various growing media and the different setups, you can start deciding which one will suit you best. Most people use expanded clay for their system because of its weight and the fact that it's easy to handle.

How to build it:

You will need an IBC container that you need to cut in two. Cut approximately 15 inches from the top, place wooden planks on top and flip the top part, so it sits on the wooden planks.

Place your preferred siphon at the base of the growbed. Fill the fish tank with water and install a pump that is able to cycle the volume of the fish tank through the system at least once an hour.

Test the siphon if it works before filling the bed with your media. Also, check for any leaks during this stage.

If the leak test passes, wash your media first to remove any dust or debris. Fill the media bed with your grow media.

Tune in the siphon according to your growbed.

Let the system cycle (more on this later in the book).

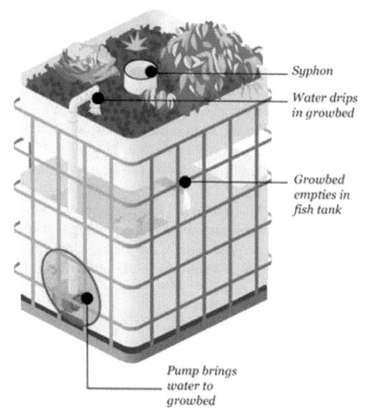

Syphon

Water drips
in growbed

Growbed
empties in
fish tank

Pump brings
water to
growbed

*The popular 'cut and flip' aquaponics IBC setup
(image by Els Engel)*

Nutrient Film Technique

We have discussed the media filled bed technique. Now we are going to look at the nutrient film technique, also called NFT.

This method is borrowed from hydroponics, where it is exceptionally popular. But it is not commonly used in aquaponics.

The growing area is essentially a collection of small gutter pipes. Each of the gutter pipes has holes cut out where a plant should be located. The plant is placed in a cup within the hole, allowing its roots to go to the bottom of the gutter and access the nutrient-rich water.

Nutrient film technique (NFT) used on a farm in Thailand

In the case of aquaponics, the wastewater from the fish passes through a solids filter and a biofilter first before flowing along the gutter pipes. Then it will go to a sump tank where it will be pumped back to the fish tank.

This is generally a good technique for plants with small roots. Any crop with a large root system is likely to clog up the water flow. Leafy green vegetables like lettuce are a popular choice with this type of setup.

Remember that in the media filled bed technique, there was a medium that houses the bacteria? In the case of the NFT method, there isn't a lot of surface area for the bacteria to settle on.

Sure, you have the walls of your fish tank and the gutters, but it really isn't that much when you compare it to a media-filled bed. That's why you need an additional biofilter. Luckily, I'm going to explain to you how to make one later in this book. A biofilter can be expensive to make. You can also use media beds as your biofilter for an NFT system.

The advantage of the NFT system is that it's ergonomically made. When you want to harvest, you don't have to bend over to access the plant like a DWC system. You can decide the height at which you want your plants to be.

A disadvantage about this system is that the small amount of water in the gutter pipes will heat up or cool down quickly, depending on the environment. Therefore, the temperature of the water will not be as stable as a DWC (deep water culture) system.

Another potential issue is solids build up. If you have floating or unfiltered solids going through your filter, it will get caught by the roots of your plants and create dirty that. The dirty particles on your roots will stick to them, preventing it from absorbing oxygen. This will lead to root rot, and eventually, your plant will suffer in growth or even die.

If the water supply is interrupted by a clog or pump failure, the roots will dry out quickly and die off before you even find the clog or have a replacement pump. I would advise against using an NFT system as a beginner because of the reasons mentioned before.

Let's review the most common commercial aquaponics system next.

Deep Water Culture

Instead of having a specific media to grow your plants in, this approach, also known as floating rafts, allows the roots of the plants to soak in the nutrient-rich water all the time.

A floating raft system doesn't use grow media like a grow bed does. Instead, the plants are placed into net pots, which are then placed into holes that are cut into Styrofoam panels (rafts). The roots of the plant will be submerged into the nutrient-rich water the whole time.

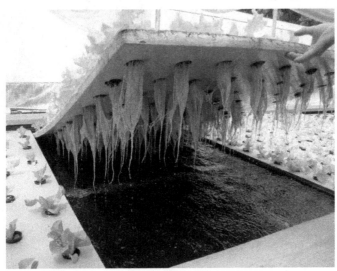

Deepwater Culture (DWC) in aquaponics

The styrofoam floats on the water, ensuring that the roots are constantly wet, the plant can have nutrients whenever it needs them.

One of the most common materials for the tray is a styrofoam or polystyrene board. The depth of the water reservoir underneath the polystyrene boards should be 10 to 12 inches.

This option is preferred for commercial growers as you can have an array of plants in different stages of growth and even pick up the boards and move them.

If you visit a commercial aquaponics farm, I'm sure you will see one of these.

Example of a commercial DWC system

If you are going to use the DWC system, you can't just use any styrofoam raft. You need to use one that's organic and not harmful to you and your fish.

Therefore, the styrofoam called 'dow blue' is a good choice and is used by many growers because it uses an environment-friendly flame-retardant technology called polymeric technology.

Here are the pros and cons of a DWC system:

Pros

- Error margin is larger (pH. levels, oxygen, etc.) because of the large amount of water.
- A large volume of water ensures stable water temperature.

Cons

- Water needs more oxygen because the roots will be submerged all the time.
- Solids build-up at the bottom of the trough could still be a problem if the solids filtration is bad.

This is how you create a small, deep-water culture setup:

Build one trough with a height of 15 inches and a length of 20 feet (length is up to you). This can be done using wooden poles and planks connecting these poles. Make sure the trough is not wider than 6 feet. If you go wider, it might be hard to reach the plants for visual checks.

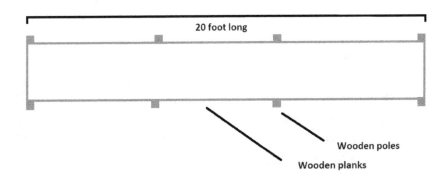

Then add a liner. It can be a cheap plastic or a more rigid (more expensive) pond liner. Then it's time to add a sump tank (lowest point in the system and partially underground).

Next, we add a pump to lift the water to the fish tank.

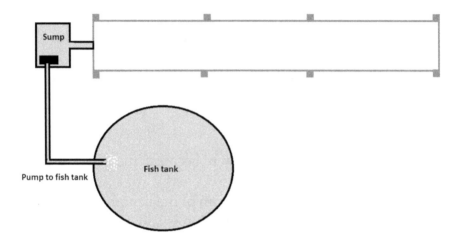

When installing the piping from the sump tank to the fish tank, you can create a small waterfall (few inches), which will oxygenate the water. You can also add a venturi, which we will discuss later.

A word about the sump:
You don't really need a sump in a DWC system. You can directly pump the water from the DWC to the fish tank. Your DWC will already be the lowest part of the system, so essentially, no sump is needed. But I included it in this example.

When the water level drops, the floating rafts will lower as a result. Because of the high volume, the drop will be minimal. Make sure to have the suction pipe of the pump mounted to the base and not like an overflow. This way, your pump doesn't run dry. See the following image.

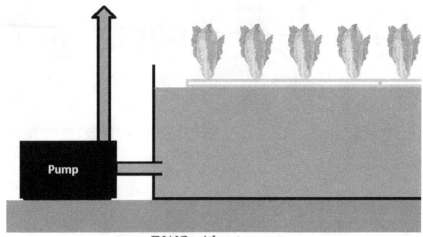
DWC without sump

Tip:
The higher your pump needs to pump the water, the less volume will be pumped. I will talk more about selecting pumps later.

Remember, we used a growbed with media to house bacteria in a flood and drain system? In a DWC system, there are two ways to create a place for bacteria to live on:

- Growbeds.
- Biofilters.

Technically you could use growbeds to house the bacteria, but in this example, I am going to use the example of using a biofilter. A biofilter requires less space.
A biofilter will house the necessary bacteria to convert ammonia and ammonium to nitrites and then nitrates. It's important that you place air stones in the biofilter because bacteria need oxygen to thrive and reproduce.

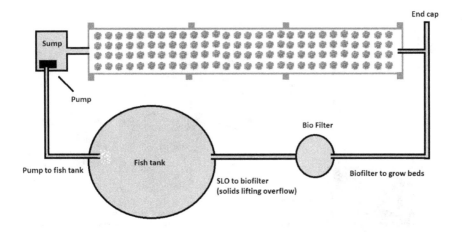

The whole system will work with one pump and two air pumps. One air pump for under the grow beds and one for the biofilter.

If you need to extend the system, you can add troughs next to it by removing the end cap and directing the overflow pipe to the sump. At the end of this book, I am going to share a few setups to inspire you to design your own DWC system.

The amount of fish you will stock depends on the total square meter of the raft area. I will explain this concept in the chapter about the biological surface area and system calculation.

It is necessary to add a solids filter between your fish tank and the biofilter (more on solid filters and separators later in the book).

Installing an SLO (solids lifting overflow) will suck up the solids from the bottom and deposit them in the solids filter (more on this later).

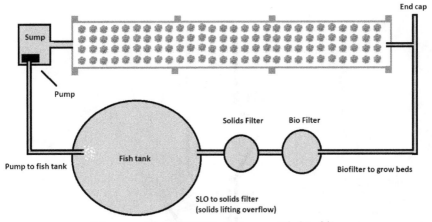

The complete DWC system with biofilter

This system is gravity fed and only requires one pump and one or more air pumps.

Vertical Towers

Vertical towers are gaining popularity in aquaponics. They use the available space efficiently. There are two kinds of vertical towers:

- Hollow towers with net pots.
- Media filled towers.

Hollow towers are vertical gutter pipes with 45 degrees angled indentation to accommodate net pots. A wick can be placed in the tower to improve the water availability to the roots. The following illustration will make the principle more clear.

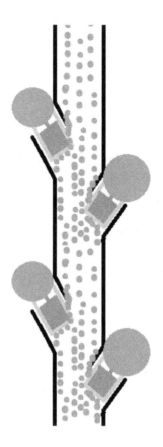

A hollow vertical tower with net pots

The water that drips in from the top of the tower needs to be checked for the tower to function. One method to make sure every plant gets the water is to install a wick throughout the tower. An example can be seen in the following illustration.

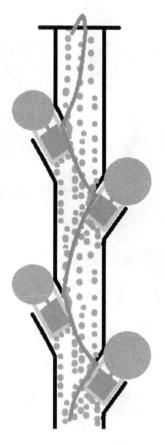

The wick makes sure water gets delivered to the roots

The other type of vertical tower is the media filled grow tower. An example of one of these towers is the zip grow tower. They use Matala mesh to hold the plants in place. It also acts as bio media because the bacteria can colonize this grow media.

A zip grow tower with grow media

The plants are placed in the towers with their roots inside the grow media. When the water trickles down on the growing media, The water gets distributed to all the roots by the growing media.

In the system designs chapter, I will give you an example of a vertical tower farm.

Dutch Buckets

Dutch buckets are very popular for a reason. They are small stand-alone grow beds. The isolation of each plant is its main purpose. Imagine having a few tomato plants in your growbed. The roots won't be contained and could clog up the siphon, create aerobic zones, and become rootbound. This will lead to your bacteria dying. Dutch buckets are mainly used for vining crops. It wouldn't make sense to plant lettuce in a dutch bucket.

Using dutch buckets allows your roots to be contained in a single bucket and isolated from the rest of the system. You will need to place another bucket next to the other in order to grow multiple plants.

You can use different grow media in dutch buckets. The best grow media for you will depend on local availability and cost. Some options are river rock, clay pebbles, or perlite, which we discussed earlier in the book.

Drip emitters are the most used form of irrigation for the dutch bucket. You can use a separate pump for your dutch buckets, which will run from the sump. Attach a drip irrigation hose to the pump and puncture the hose where you want your drip irrigation to be at, just like a drip system in a garden.

Drip emitters

You can also use regular PVC piping with valves to control the flow to each bucket. If you don't install valves on each bucket, you won't give every bucket the same amount of water. You can use a timer and turn it on 3-5 times a day for a few minutes.

You will need to use a split-flow if you use another system like growbeds.

This is what cross-section of a dutch bucket looks like:

Water supply line

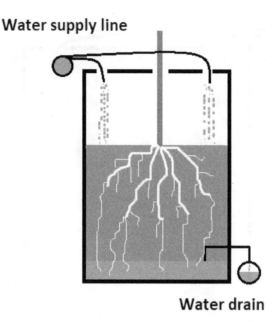

Water drain

A cross-section of a dutch bucket

The bottom two inches of the bucket will be permanently underwater. This way, the roots have a constant supply of water, but there is still enough air for the roots to avoid root rot. If you are using perlite, you can imagine it being washed away in the drain. That's why you should use coarser rocks at the bottom to aid in drainage and prevent smaller particles from exiting. The drain pipe will be one inch in diameter and can have a net pot to prevent coarse material from washing away.

You can also use mesh bags to keep the perlite contained. It's easier to clean the buckets after the harvest.

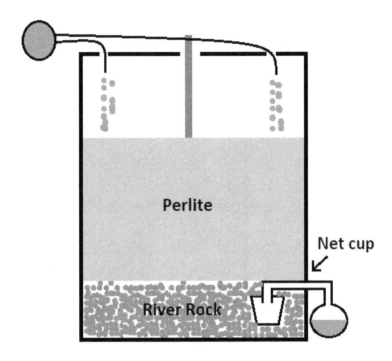

Using a net cup and coarse media at the bottom for better drainage

Don't rely on including the biological surface area (BSA) of the dutch buckets to your system. They are not constantly flooded and drained. Thus not a lot of bacteria will be on the surface of the media. Always use a growbed or biofilter in combination with dutch buckets.

Several of these buckets are placed after each other depending on nutrient availability in your system. If your system is running low on nitrates, consider increasing the feed to your fish or don't plant as many fruiting crops. Installing trellises will help vining crops to develop optimally.

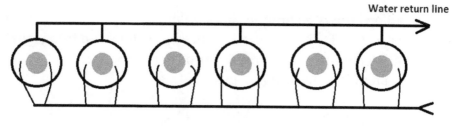

A chain of Dutch buckets with drip irrigation

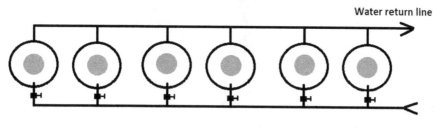

A chain of Dutch buckets with valve-controlled flow

The water supply line comes from either your sump tank or directly after your solids filter or biofilter. Most of the time, dutch buckets are added at a later stage when the system has matured. I have included such a set up in the system designs chapter at the end of this book.

DTF (Deep Flow Technique)

The deep flow technique is similar to the nutrient film technique (NFT). The only difference between these two is that the DFT technique has more water in the channels.
This system has two advantages:

- Pump failure:
  In a classic NFT system, when a pump failure happens, you usually have a few hours to a day to fix it. If the pump fails in a DFT system, the roots still have access to water.

- Lower temperature changes:
  Because there is more water running in the system, the water temperature in a DFT system is less likely to fluctuate much during day and night.

But there is also a disadvantage:

- Oxygen:
  The roots will be submerged in the water. To prevent root rot from happening, your water needs to be well oxygenated.

In a way, you can compare the DFT to a DWC system. But with DFT, you have the option to go vertical. The water in a DFT system needs to be properly oxygenated in order for the plants to thrive in this environment. You do this by installing air stones in your fish tank. It's possible to install air stones in the channels, but you would have a hard time placing them and supplying all the airlines, let alone doing maintenance. In my opinion, it is better to put them in the fish tank.

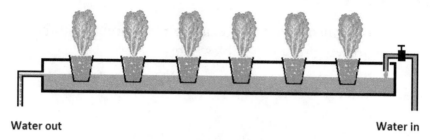

Water out   **Water in**

Simplified DTF system

In this image, the tube is a 3 inch PVC pipe with 2-inch holes drilled with a hole saw. The holes should be 8 inches apart from each other for lettuce (center to center). The water coming in is controlled by a valve on each PVC pipe; this is to make sure other channels have the same flow rate.

To drain the water, you can use a 3-inch end cap for the PCV piping. Drill a hole just above the middle of the end cap and insert a one inch PVC pipe. Then, seal it with silicone or PVC glue. The height of the water in the PVC pipe should be around 1½ inches if you are using a 3-inch pipe.

You can use DFT as a vertical growing method or a horizontal method. If you have the space available, I recommend using a horizontal setup if space is not a limiting factor. It's more ergonomic, easier to build, and plants get more light.

Wicking beds

Wicking beds also called SIP beds (Self Irrigating Plant bed) is a way of growing root vegetables like:

- Potatoes.
- Radishes.
- Carrots.

The idea is to have a water reservoir at the bottom of a raised bed, which will be wicked up to the roots of the root crop. The wicking bed is completely lined with pond liner to prevent moisture from escaping. You can use your own composting mix as the soil. Make sure the soil you add can wick the water.

The base of the bed is filled with river rock. The river rock is separated from the growing media with a weed barrier. This prevents dirt from going down and getting in between the river rock. The bottom part is always flooded.

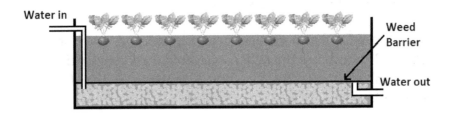

Cross-section of a wicking bed

An even simpler wicking bed method can be used. You would still line the raised bed with a liner to prevent moisture from escaping. But this time, you just let the water evaporate. You would only need to open the ball valve to the wicking bed maybe once a week. You can regulate the height of the water in the bed. Just make sure the water level is still below the main root mass, or they will rot.

Simplified wicking bed

The water will be entering the bed but will not recirculate back to the aquaponics system. You can look at the water level in the wicking bed through the standing pipe and turn the ball valve on or off. This method is not as complex as the previous one.

Essential Items

Aquaponics will be as complicated as you want it to be. Getting started is surprisingly straightforward. All you need is basic knowledge from this book, the items on this list, and the willingness to try aquaponics without having everything perfect for the first time.

Your Plan

This is an often-overlooked part of any aquaponics system. Before you can start getting your supplies together, you need to think about what it is; you are hoping to achieve.

- Do you want to grow lettuce or bigger fruiting plants?
- Do you want to use a media bed or a DWC system?
- What's the location like? (sunshine)
- What's the climate like?
- Where can I get my fish from?
- Can I find these supplies nearby?
- How much room do I have available?

Fish Tank

You will need something to keep your fish in. You can start with a conventional fish tank or a rigid pond liner. Pretty much anything that can hold water can be used for this part of the system.

However, the size of the fish tank does matter. Your tank needs to be sized to the amount of fish and plants you want. We'll look at this shortly. Popular options for fish tanks are:

- IBC tote (cubic container).
- Solid plastic tubs.
- Existing pond.
- Specially designed fish tanks with conical bottom.
- Big fiberglass fish tanks.

Classic IBC tote

Before you use any fish tank, make sure you clean them out. If you decide to use an IBC, you need to make sure it is food graded. You don't want any nasty chemicals in your system. Always ask the owner what the previous content was.

If you can't write down or memorize the name of its previous content, it is a good idea to move on to the next supplier. You can find suppliers on eBay or at a farm nearby. Farmers use them to supply water to their livestock.

When you get an IBC tote or any other fish tank, you should paint it black to avoid algae from growing on the inside walls. You can finish it with a layer of white paint on top in case the sun hits it directly.

Always choose a fish tank where it will be easy to get rid of the solids at the bottom. A big plastic swimming pool might be a great idea, but removing the solids from the bottom will be not as easy. An IBC tote is the perfect container to start with.

Grow Bed

A grow bed is essentially a large tray that is used to grow plants. It should be filled with media such as gravel, lava rocks, river rocks, or other media. In addition to the standard task of growing plants, the growbed also acts as a biofilter, solids filter, and mineralization

You can opt for one grow bed or several. These are where the plants will be growing. Ideally, they should be approximately 12 inches deep.

The bed doesn't need anything additional except for an entry and exit point for your water. The entry of the water is from the top, and the exit is from the bottom using one of the siphoning systems.

Here are some ideas for media filled beds:

- The top part of the IBC (15 inches high).
- Boxes made with wood and pond liner.
- 55-gallon barrels cut in half.
- A plastic tub.

The water coming in from the fish tank should be evenly distributed across the surface of the growbed. Failing to do so will create concentrated pockets of solid fish waste.

55-gallon barrels as media bed (barrelponics)

Distributing the solids evenly

Pump

You will need a pump to move the water from the fish tank to the grow beds. A simple electric pump is all it takes.

You must design your system in such a way that it uses as little electricity as possible. In other words, you must:

- Let gravity do its job.
- Limit head height.

In most commercial systems, the water gets pumped from the sump to the fish tank. Gravity will then take the water through the filters, biofilter, and DWC troughs before entering the sump to repeat the cycle all over again.

However, as this is an integral part of the system, it is worth getting a spare pump; in case you have any issues with your main one. I will talk about how to place two pumps in parallel in the 'advanced techniques' chapter.

Next, I'm going to talk about how you should select a pump.

What is your desired flow rate?
You will decide the flow rate of your aquaponics system by the fact that the water in your fish tank needs to be recirculated at least once an hour.

If you use the advanced IBC setup that I show you at the end of the book, you would need to have a pump with a rating of at least 250 gallons per hour.

But this rating alone is not enough. There is something called 'head height' of a pump, which you need to consider as well.

How high do you need to pump?

The next question is how high you need to pump your water to whatever system you are using. If you are pumping from a sump to the fish tank, you can have a few feet of head height.

When you are designing your system, you need to design it in a way that there is not much head height. Less head height will require less energy consumption, which means money saved. In the following image, you can see what head height really is. Now, decide what your head height will be of your system and keep that in mind for the following step.

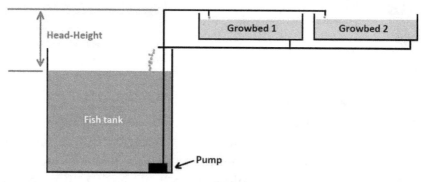

Calculating head height

What is the head height of a pump?

Let's say you bought the 250 gallon per hour pump for your IBC system. The pump tells you it is 250 gallons per hour so it should pump 250 gallons per hour in my growbeds, right?

Not exactly,

You see, the flow rate of a pump is described with zero feet of head height (elevation). This means the pump will deliver 250 gallons per hour without lifting it up to your growbeds. The flow rate will decrease once you are pumping the water up.

Luckily there are charts available for a pump that will indicate flow rate with a certain amount of head height. Below you can see such a curve which is called 'a pump curve,' which puts the relation between flow rate and head height in a nice graph.

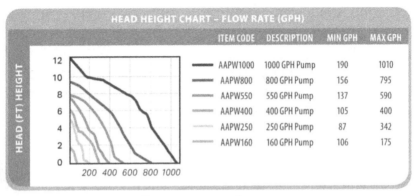

6 pump curves in one

Reading the pump curve

Every decent manufacturer or seller will have a pump curve in its user manual or datasheet. If you can't find it on their website, try to search for: 'name of pump + user manual,' and with a bit of luck, you should see a pdf file with a pump curve.

Once you have found the pump curve of the pump you want to use, you need to look at the left axis first. Find the head height you calculated for your system and draw a line to the right. Next, look for your required minimum flow rate and draw a vertical line. The point where these lines cross is your pump 'working' point.

In this example, it's right on the 400 GPH pump line.

If your working point is between two pump lines, you need to move up to the right. Never go to the left because you won't make the recommended minimum one-hour recycling time of the water.

You always need to oversize your pump because it's better to pump the water around more than once an hour instead of less.

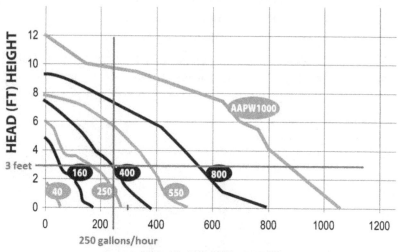

GALLONS PER HOUR (LPH) VOLUME

You need a pump of 400 gallons/hour

In the image above, I used an example of an IBC as a fish tank with some grow beds next to it. The volume of the IBC will be around 250 gallons (fully topped). The point where the two lines cross will be your desired pump flow rate. As you can see, if we would have taken the 250 gallons/hour pump, we wouldn't make it to 250 gallons per hour (we would be pumping 180 gallons/hour).

Instead, we choose for the 400 gallons per hour pump if we want to pump at least 250 gallons per hour with a head height of 3 feet.

Seed Starter Cubes

I use Rockwool cubes to start the seeds. More specifically, the grow blocks from grodan. Using seed starting sponges is very cheap but not very environmentally friendly.

Take a seed starter cube and soak it at a pH of 6. You can also use the water of your aquaponics system if it has a low pH. Don't squeeze the cubes because you will crush the air pockets inside the cube.

Seed starter cubes from grodan

Put your seeds in the wet starter cube and cover it with a few Rockwool fibers. Then, place them in a tray with a humidity dome over it to keep it humid inside.

Next, place them in a dark place for around 3 days. Water once every day from the bottom, so the Rockwool cubes stay moist. Aim for a temperature between 60 and 65°F for lettuce seedlings (15-18°C) and a humidity of 60%+.

When you see a few inches of growth and the first two leaves developing, it's time to remove the humidity dome and transplant them to the system.

For media beds, you can just place them right on the flood line. For DWC and NFT, you need to place them in net pots.

Place an inch of media (I prefer hydroton) at the bottom of the net pot. Place the seed starter cube in the middle and fill in the sides with some additional hydroton. You don't need to cover the top with hydroton, just enough to keep the starter cubes in place.

Some people place two seeds per seeding hole. I don't bother because it takes time to remove the second one if they both have sprouted. If they don't sprout, I use the cubes again next time.

Example of a seedling tray with dome

Pipe Work

You will need several sets of pipes, connectors, bulkheads, uniseals, and ball valves to join your fish tank to your grow bed and then return the water back to the fish tank.

For a small system (less than 200 gallons), you would use ½ inch diameter pipework. But if your system will get bigger (200 gallons+), you will need to use 1 inch or bigger.

Flexible polyethylene can be used for small systems like the cut and flip IBC setup.

You can use PEX with 'push to connect' valves and connectors. Shark bite fittings, couplings, and valves are also popular.

SharkBite push and connect ball-valve for PEX

PVC piping is a good alternative to flexible polyethylene and PEX. You will need to make accurate measurements before cutting the pipe.

The most used piping for aquaponics is the standard non-flexible PVC pipe. There are many reducers, connectors, and ball valves available in your local hardware store. I recommend using this kind for your piping. Some people don't glue their pipes at all. I recommend to at least glue the pressure pipe. That is the pipe that is attached to your pump.

Don't use transparent piping because the inside will encourage algae growth.

SLO

You need to use an SLO (solids lifting overflow) to suck up the solids from the bottom of your fish tank. I recommend everyone to install an SLO.

This is how it works:

The fish create waste, and it drops to the bottom of your tank. If you use an overflow in your fish tank without an SLO, the solids will stay at the bottom. It will become a dirty and toxic environment for your fish.

We need to figure out a way of getting rid of the solids down at the bottom.

We do this by creating a standing pipe in your fish tank. The standing pipe should be approximately one inch from the bottom. There should be an end cap drilled with small holes, so the fish don't get sucked in. It basically acts like a vacuum for the bottom of your tank.

The pipe then goes up to a T-piece where the top will be open. The open-top prevents the fish tank from emptying during a power cut because of the siphon effect.

The other part of the T-piece should be connected to a pipe that goes outside at the same height you want the water level to be. Bulkhead fitting or uniseals are used to seal off the outlet from the fish tank. I recommend a uniseal because there is not a lot of pressure at the top of the water, and it is cheaper.

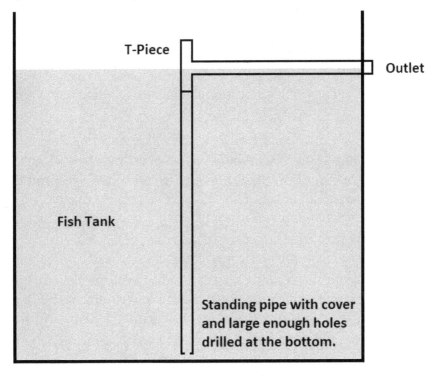

Solids lifting overflow

The bigger the diameter of the pipe, the slower the water will move. The slower the water moves, the less suction it has, which will result in failure to suck up the heavy solids.

I do not advise to go any larger than 2 inches on any setup.

If you have a 500-gallon tank, you don't need a 4-inch pipe. The water will just flow at a faster rate. The maximum SLO I recommend is 2 inches combined with a bypass, which I will talk about later in the book.

Having the return line from your pump going in a circular direction will create a vortex and collect the solids in the middle of the fish tank. This will make it easier to suck up the solids.

The fish that swim near the bottom will stir up the solids, which will increase the chance of being sucked up by the SLO.

Aerator

Your fish, plants, and bacteria need oxygen to survive. An aerator, such as the type you use in any fish tank, will ensure they have the oxygen they need to survive and complete the system.

You need to use an air stone combined with your air pump to add oxygen. Air stones are porous stones that diffuse the air and allow it to be effectively released into your tank or biofilter. The smaller the air bubbles, the more effective the aeration.

You can check if your fish need more oxygen by observing how they behave. If they are gasping for air at the surface, it shows you need to add more air in the water.

The available air in the water (dissolved oxygen) will decrease when water temperature increases. During winter, you might have enough oxygen, but during summer, your fish might be oxygen-deprived.

A typical air stone

The deeper you put the stones under the water surface, the less air that will be diffused. This is because the air has more resistance when it's placed on the bottom.

Where do you place the air stone?

- In a flood and drain system, you place the air stone in your fish tank.

- In an NFT system, you place the air stone in your biofilter and fish tank.

- For DWC, you need to place air stones in your biofilter (if you don't use growbeds), in your fish tank, and under the floating rafts to provide oxygen to the roots.

It is possible to add air to the water by disturbing the water surface when the water returns to the tank. This needs to be considered as an addition and should not be relied on.

In the following image, you see an SLO and a return line with small holes providing more aeration to the water. The way the return line and the small holes are set up is to let the water move like a vortex, drawing the solids to the center for the SLO to pick up.

Additional aeration (image from aquaponiclynx.com)

Grow Lights

Depending on where you are placing your setup, you may decide that your plants will benefit from some extra light.

Grow lights are the best way to do this because they have the light spectrum that the plants like. The lights you get in the hardware store are designed for households and do not give you the desired intensity (lumens) or light spectrum (kelvin).

Light spectrum
In this image, you can see the light spectrum using the Kelvin scale:

Colour Temperatures in the Kelvin Scale

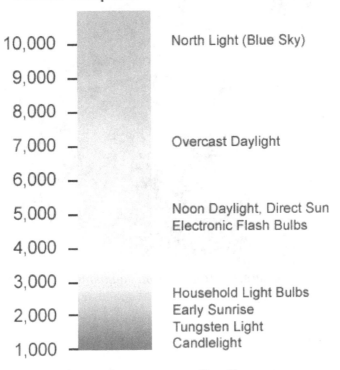

10,000 –	North Light (Blue Sky)
9,000 –	
8,000 –	
7,000 –	Overcast Daylight
6,000 –	
5,000 –	Noon Daylight, Direct Sun Electronic Flash Bulbs
4,000 –	
3,000 –	
2,000 –	Household Light Bulbs Early Sunrise Tungsten Light
1,000 –	Candlelight

Image from www.mediacollege.com

If you go shopping for a grow light, you will have two dominant choices. Buying cool blue lights (6500K) or warm red lights (4000K).

For seedlings and vegetative growth, it is best to use the cool blue light. Plants use this light to create energy to grow. Use these for leafy crops like lettuce, kale, basil, etc.

The other light spectrum is warm red light. These are used for growing fruiting crops like strawberries, tomatoes, etc. The red light will make sure the fruit the plant produces is big. If the plant lacks the red spectrum, the produced fruits will be smaller.

Tomatoes are grown with two different light spectrums if grown indoors. First, cool blue light to develop leaves and warm red to produce the tomatoes themselves.

Light intensity

The intensity of light is also important. The higher the intensity of the light, the more energy it provides to the plant. The unit of light intensity is lumens.

The higher the intensity, the farther away you need to suspend it from the plant, covering a bigger grow area. You can say lumens is the unit of light quantity delivered to a plant.

Light duration (photoperiod)

The light duration depends on the plant itself. Different plants have different needs for light duration. Lettuce, for example, has a recommended minimum light duration of 12 hours a day. This means, to optimally grow lettuce, you should expose it to light for at least 12 hours each day.

The light duration during the life cycle of a plant can change. For example, the light duration where tomatoes are in their vegetative stage will be different than their fruiting stage.

DLI (daily light integral)

The DLI or daily light integral is the amount of light a plant receives in one day per square meter. Each plant has a recommended DLI. If you are growing outdoors, you can look at a map, which lists the DLI in different parts of the USA. https://www.howtoaquaponic.com/DLI-USA

You need to have a light that delivers the daily amount of DLI to the plant in their specific light duration. Any DLI that is over the recommended DLI would be a waste of energy because plants have light saturation. This means that plants can't absorb more light per day.

Recommended DLI values:
- leafy greens: 10-25 mol/m²/day
- flowering crops: 25-35 mol/m²/day

Calculating DLI

You need to calculate your DLI to get the most efficient power usage for the most crop growth. I am going to use lettuce with T5 fluorescents as an example to grow lettuce in a one square meter growbed (cut and flip IBC).

We know that lettuce likes a DLI of 12-14 mol/m²/day. Next, we need to know how many lumens our grow light has. You can find this on the data sheet of the light. The one I'm using has 5000 lumens per 4ft T5 tube, which I found on amazon.

Next, we will convert the lumens to PPF, which will give us umol/s (micro mols per second). I do this by using the following calculator:
https://www.waveformlighting.com/horticulture/convert-lumens-to-ppf-online-calculator

I select the light color, which is cool blue or daylight (6500K), and insert the lumens, which one 4ft T5 light will emit.

Convert Lumens to PPF - Online Calculator

Lumens: 5000

Spectrum: Natural Daylight 6500K   ▾

Calculate

Result: 115 umol/s

Conversion from lumens to PPF

We have a result of 115 umol/s. Next, I use another calculator, which will convert PPFD (umol/s/m²) to DLI (mol).

You see that the unit of PPFD is not the same as the previously calculated PPF. This is because PPFD is measured per square meter. But since we are growing our lettuce in one square meter, we can say they are equal.

Use the following calculator:
https://www.waveformlighting.com/horticulture/daily-light-integral-dli-calculator

If we input our previous result of 115 umol/s and the recommended light duration for lettuce, we become 4.97. This is not enough for our lettuce to grow efficiently.

DLI with one T5 tube

We need a DLI of at least 12 for the lettuce to grow well. If I use more lights, I will get to the recommended DLI of 12. I multiply the PPFD by 3:

$$115x3 = 345$$

Because I am going to use 3 T5 light tubes. When we run the calculator again, we become a DLI of 14.9, which is slightly too high.

A DLI that is too high will result in wasted energy.

PPFD (umol/s/m2) to DLI (mol) Calculator

PPFD (umol/s/m2): **345**

Time (hours): **12**

Calculate

Result: DLI = 14.90

DLI is too high

Now we have two options:

- Increase the light duration
- Decrease the amount of T5 tubes

In this case, I choose to decrease the amount of T5 tubes to two and play with the light duration to reach a DLI of 12.

The final result

The final setup would be to use two 4ft T5 tubes per square meter to grow lettuce at a light interval of 14 and a half-hour a day.

The T5 light uses 54 watts per tube. Total cost of running this setup would be:

$$54\ watts\ x\ 2 = 108\ watts\ total$$

$$14.5\ hours\ x\ 108\ watts = 1566\ watt\ hours\ per\ day$$

$$\frac{1566\ watt\ hours\ per\ day}{1000} = 1.566k\ watt\ hours\ per\ day$$

Using the national average of \$0.12 per kilowatt-hour, we become:

$$1.566kwh\ x\ \$0.12\ = \$0.187\ per\ day\ or\ \$68.5\ per\ year$$

If we decided to use 3 bulbs and decrease the light interval, we would have a similar electricity cost. I choose to buy only two T5 tube fixtures because two are cheaper than three. The light tube itself is cheaper to replace (has an average 20,000 hours lifespan= 4 years running at 14.5 hours a day).

LEDs
They are the most efficient kind of lights to use when your head clearance is limited. They can provide all the light spectrums you want. They are very versatile but come at a price point. In my opinion, it is not worth the upfront cost of LEDs for the hobbyist.

If the place you are growing is hot and it is hard to get rid of heat, I would recommend LEDs.

Fluorescents
Fluorescents, on the other hand, are a good and cheap alternative to LEDs. Choose the more efficient T5 tubes. They come in 2 or 4 feet long. In my opinion, this is the best grow light to use for the hobbyist.

Other lights
High-pressure sodium is mostly used in a greenhouse with a lot of head clearance. They can supplement the light of a plant very effectively. You can't use high-pressure sodium lights close to a plant because it is very intense (high lumens) and produces quite some heat that can burn your plants.

Testing Equipment

The main test you will be completing is pH level checks. This can be done with a simple pH meter. Don't use testing strips because they are quite inaccurate. The main items you need to test are:

- pH.
- Ammonia.
- Nitrite.
- Nitrate.
- Oxygen.
- Iron.
- EC.
- Temperature.

The depth of your testing will depend on how serious you want to get.

As part of this, you will need to have some pH adjusters; this will enable you to change the pH to the right level when needed. Don't increase or decrease the pH by more than 0.5 a day to reduce stress to the fish and plants.

When your system is established, it is rare to have a high pH level. If you do, it is probably a result of carbonate build-up. This is usually connected with limestone in your tank or the use of hard water. I will talk later about lowering your pH.

You often hear people say that adding lemon juice to your system to get the pH levels down. Don't do this! The acid will kill your bacteria and lockout other nutrients!

Electrical Conductivity (EC)

An electrical conductivity meter or EC is used to measure the nutrients that are present in your system. The unit of EC is milli Siemens per centimeter (mS/cm).

An EC meter measures the amount of dissolved nutrients in the water. There are all kinds of nutrients dissolved in the water like nitrates, phosphorus, potassium, calcium, boron, iron, manganese.

All these dissolved nutrients represent the total EC level. If you have a high EC level, many of these nutrients are dissolved in the water. If you have a low EC level, fewer nutrients are dissolved.

Nutrients are basically electrolytes. Electrolytes are salts that will conduct electricity. The meter measures the resistance the water has when a small current is put through it (not dangerous to the fish). The higher the salt content (electrolytes), the higher the EC number.

Some plants require higher EC than others. For example, seedlings and lettuce can grow perfectly with a low EC (1) while fruiting crops need a high EC. Each plant has its recommended EC range.

If you manually add salt to your system, the EC reading will become inaccurate. It is, therefore, only usable in a salt-free system.

The EC level will increase if the water gets warmer. When you are growing in warm areas, it is important to lower the EC. The higher the EC measurement, the higher the ion or electrolyte level. If the EC is getting high, your low EC plants like lettuce can't absorb water and nutrients efficiently. If the temperature rises, and you are growing plants like lettuce, you need to lower the EC.

I was visiting a lettuce aquaponics farm in Thailand, and they lower their EC to 1 when summer starts. When the summer ends, and it is getting cooler, they allow their EC to rise again but not above 1.5.

EC meters do not read every nutrient, so it is still important to do your routine water checks. They can be quite expensive for the hobbyist and is mainly used in commercial systems. The Groline EC meter is a good one. It also measures pH; temperature, and you can set several alarms.

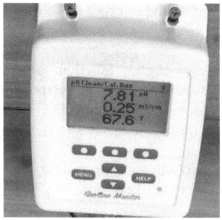

Groline EC meter with pH and temperature measurements

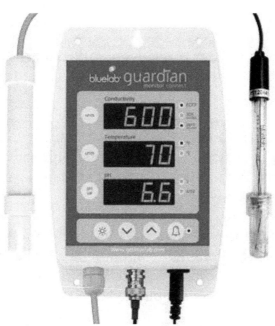

Bluelab Guardian EC meter combined with pH and temperature

An EC meter can't measure a single nutrient deficiency because it can only measure the total amount of nutrients. You still need to observe your plants for specific nutrient deficiencies, which we will talk about later.

Timers

If you plan to use grow lights, you need to use a simple timer. Hours of light exposure depends on the kind of plant and its growing stage.

You also need a timer when you decide to use the timed flood and drain option, which I discussed in the media bed systems.

Water

The aquaponic system is relatively self-contained. Other than some regular water testing, visual checks, and fish food, it should take care of itself.

If you are filling your system for the first time, you don't need to filter it. Rainwater is perfect for this. Alternatively, you can use tap water, but it needs to aerate for a few days to get rid of the chlorine in the water.

Chloramine is the new chlorine. Most distributors are moving from chlorine to chloramine. Chloramine can't be aired out and needs to be removed using a carbon or reverse osmosis filter. Check your local water supplier what they use in the water.

Be careful with well water. Make sure to check the hardiness of the water before you put it in your system. I will talk more about the recommended water hardness later.

Using water from an existing pond will be the best option. Along with some bio-media to jumpstart the bacterial growth.

Fish Food

You will need fish food, and it is best to get one that gives your fish all the nutrition they need in an easily identifiable quantity. Organic high protein fish food is preferred. If the surface of your water is oily, it probably means that your food isn't great and contains a lot of fat.

Feeding them too much can cause a buildup of waste. This leads to solids on the bottom of your fish tank, or your grow bed being full of solids.

The general fish feeding rate is 0.2 to 0.32 ounces of fish food a day per square foot of growing area (60-100grams/m²). This rate is used for optimal plant growth in the DWC aquaponics system.

For growbeds, this is 15-40 grams/m² of growing area that is 1ft deep.

Solids Removal

While the bacteria will do a good job of processing the ammonia to nitrates, they don't remove the solid waste from the fish. To prevent the excess solids from building up in your system, you need a good filter or solids separation system.

The best place to do this is right after the water leaves the fish tank. If you have a small IBC setup with one grow bed, it is not necessary because the grow bed itself will act as a solids filter and mineralization. In this case, the fish waste will be limited (if you use the specified feeding ratio).

If you don't have solids filtration in a small setup, I highly recommend using earthworms in the growbeds. Earthworms eat the solids, which will break them down to worm castings, which contains usable nutrients for your plants.

If you have a high-density system, you should install a solids filter or separator because your system will get full of fish waste. If you don't use a solids filter with high stocking densities in combination with media beds, expect to clean them out at least once every year.

If the earthworms can't process all the fish waste, the solids will build up in the grow bed and create zones without oxygen (anaerobic). These zones will prevent bacteria from colonizing them, resulting in less available biofiltration.

If your test results come back with high pH after your system was stable, you should check for solids build up in your growbed. I will explain more about the relationship between ammonia and pH later in the book.

When you are using floating rafts (DWC), vertical towers, or NFT, solids filters become increasingly important. Why?

In these kinds of systems, there is no place for the solids to get processed by earthworms.

If you don't have solids separation in a deep-water culture system, NFT, or any other system, the solids will deposit somewhere. This will result in dirty roots and a layer of fish solids in the system.

Furthermore, the solids will hinder the roots from taking up the much-needed oxygen, which will result in root rot and a dying plant. It is important to have a good solids filtration or separation when you are running any setup without media beds.

I have seen commercial DWC setups where the water from the fish tank goes through a settler first to get rid of the settable (heavy) solids first, and then to a media bed to remove the rest of the solids. Then it is run to the floating rafts by gravity. This is a very good method of solids removal.

Heavy solids get captured in the filter and move on to a mineralization tank. The smaller solids that manage to get past the filter get trapped in the media beds and are getting processed by the earthworms. This will lead to very clean water in the DWC troughs.

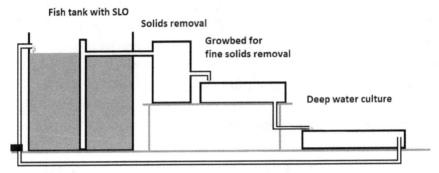

Growbeds for suspended solids removal in a DWC system

There are different solids removal methods. A solids filter will filter out the solids, and a solids separator will separate the solids. Both are doing the same, but both use different methods.

A separator uses the motion of the water to let the solids settle at the bottom of the tank. Three examples of a separator are:

- A swirl separator.
- A vortex separator.
- A radial flow separator.

When you are using a separator, there is one variable that's very important. It is called retention or detention time. This is the total time the water will be in the separator. You need to aim for at least 20 minutes in your solid's separator.

For example, you have a flow rate of 150 gallons per hour and a 50-gallon solids separator. This means you have a retention time of 20 minutes. This is the minimum recommended retention time.

If you have a flow rate of 300 gallons per hour, but you have the same 50-gallon solids separator, your retention time will decrease to only 10 minutes. This is not enough time for the solids to settle at the bottom. In this case, you need to:

- **Install a bigger separator**: this speaks for itself. The bigger the volume, the longer the retention time.
- **Divert a part of the flow** (more on this in the advanced chapter).
- **Install another separator in parallel**: this will split the flow and divide the flow rate in two. Take a look at the following image:

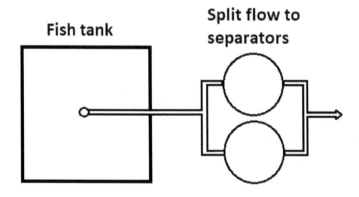

Splitting the flow into two solid separators

It is important to install them in parallel, as shown in the image. If you put them in series (after each other), you would still have the same retention time because the flow isn't divided. Let's move on to showing you a few solid separators.

Here are some of the separators you can use in your aquaponics system:

Swirl separator

The swirl filter is also called a vortex. Most of the time, these are barrels with a cone-like shape at the bottom. The incoming pipe will be coming into the barrel in the middle, directing the flow to create a swirl (like a tornado). The speed of the water will force the solids that are heavier than the water to settle down at the bottom.

The clean water that is free of heavy solids will then go through the pipe in the middle to the next stage of your setup (usually a biofilter or grow beds). Occasionally you need to open the valve at the bottom of the swirl separator to get rid of the solids. You can use the solids as a fertilizer for your garden (not in your aquaponics system) or send them to your mineralization tank.

The classic types like the one in the picture below are available in pond stores.

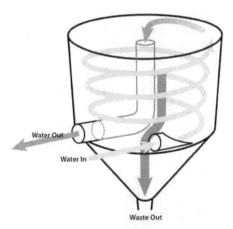

Swirl separator illustration by koilog

However, they can be expensive. It might be more fun and fulfilling to make them yourself. You can do this by using a 55-gallon drum (food graded).

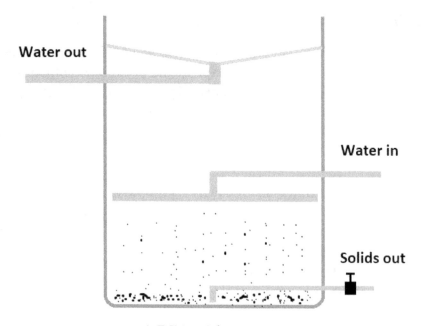

A DIY swirl separator

The 'solids out' pipe will force the particles to go through the tube using the force of the water pushing down on it (like an SLO). It works like a vacuum and needs to be shut off by a valve.

See the following picture on how to create a swirl with the incoming water.

Creating the swirl

Radial flow separator

A radial flow separator is another way for the solids to settle at the bottom of a tank. In this case, the tank is a 55-gallon drum. The water comes in but can't get directly to the outflow pipe. It first must travel through the bigger pipe in the middle.

This will allow for solids to collect at the bottom of the drum. When the solids collect on the bottom of the drum, you need to open the solids valve, and it will suck up any particles that are on the bottom.

If you have a smaller system and don't want to use a 55-gallon drum, you can still use a smaller 5-gallon bucket (only in very small systems).

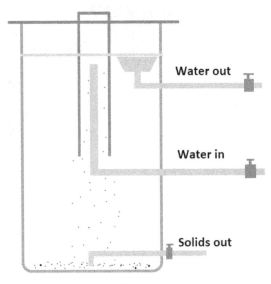

A Radial flow separator

Clarifier

A clarifier is another way of solids separation. Here, the separator is divided into two equal chambers with a separator plate in the middle. There is a gap at the bottom, which is one foot from the bottom.

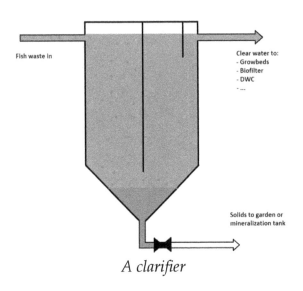

A clarifier

The water is forced to go under the separator plate, which will deposit the solids at the bottom. This method of solids removal is used by the UVI system (university of the Virgin Islands). When they drained the solids from the clarifier, it went to a mineralization tank to break down the solids to turn it into usable nutrients for the plants.

The clarifier in the UVI system

Your clarifier doesn't need to have a conical bottom. You can make one yourself using a 55-gallon drum. Use a plastic separator plate (diffuser) to divert the flow. You can attach it to the sides of the drum with silicone. Install a valve at the bottom to flush out the solids to your garden or mineralization tank.

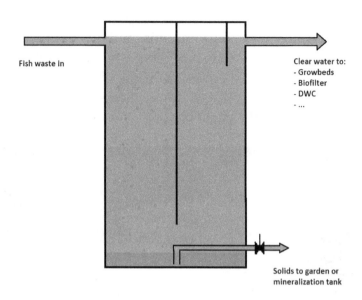

Fish waste in

Clear water to:
- Growbeds
- Biofilter
- DWC
- ...

Solids to garden or
mineralization tank

DIY clarifier in a 55-gallon drum

A filter uses mechanical filtration instead of waiting for the solids to settle. Examples of solid filters are:

- Raft filters.
- Mesh filters.
- Bead filters.

Raft Filters

This is basically a box with a few layers of vertical filtration mesh (Matala) in it.

You can use 3 types of density for the filtration mesh. The first one has the biggest spacing and the last one the least amount of spacing.

The problem with this kind of filter is that it can clog up quite quickly. If you are planning to use this filter, which I don't recommend, you need an overflow in case the mats get clogged up.

A DIY raft filter

It can be helpful only to remove one filter mat at a time; this will ensure the system keeps working while you clean the filter mats.

Simple mesh filter

A simple mesh filter will get some of the solids out of the system. Simply hang a mesh bag around the outlet of your pipe, so the water needs to go through the mesh bag first before entering the grow bed.

I don't recommend relying on mesh filters for a big system because they clog up rapidly.

The bigger solids will get broken down into smaller particle sizes because of the water that is pouring on it. The smaller particle sizes will pass through the filter and end up in your system.

They are quite maintenance-intensive. I would opt for a swirl separator, radial flow separator, or clarifier instead. But they are worth mentioning to use them for very small systems or as an addition to another filtration system.

They are also good for checking how many solids are leaving your main filtration system.

Simple mesh bag filters

Bead Filter

A bead filter is not widely used in aquaponics because it is expensive. You can't quickly make one yourself. These are two of the main reasons why they are not very popular with DIY aquaponics. Their main use is in koi ponds. The main selling point for the bead filter is that it acts both as a solids filter and a biofilter.

Installing a bead filter without any other solids' removal will put a lot of stress on the bead filter. As a result, you would need to backwash it very often. It is better to have some other solids separator before it to get rid of the bigger solids.

I will explain how they work:

A bead filter is a pressurized chamber that contains thousands of tiny plastic beads. These beads act as a biological surface area for your bacteria to live on (more about this later). The water is pumped through the filter, and the beads will capture the fish solids.

After a while, the solids inside the pressurized chamber will start to build up. To remove the solids from the bead filter, you will have to isolate the filter from the system. You do this by using a multi-way valve. Then you turn on the air pump that will blow air from the bottom into the beads. This will loosen up the solids from the beads, and the solids will float to the top. Then you open the waste valve to release the solids from the filter with the help of additional water from your system. The solids will drain to your mineralization tank or garden.

When you don't see any more solids exiting the drain valve, you can put the multi-way valve back to its original position and continue the usual operation.

A bead filter

Extras

There are a variety of extra bits that you will need when running your aquaponics system. For example, a net is extremely useful if you are trying to catch fish. I know, I have tried to get them out with tubs and all sorts of other items!

If you have lively fish like trout or tilapia, it is best to place some bird netting over your fish tank to prevent them from jumping out.

Also, if you see a fish with parasites on it, remove the sick fish from the rest asap and place it in quarantine. It is better to have the fish in quarantine before it infects the others.

It is a good idea to have some basic gardening tools. Although it can be easy to forget your plants in the excitement of your fish growing and the aquaponics system working, you will need to maintain the plants as well.

You can introduce beneficial insects to control any destructive pests.

The following insects are considered to be beneficial:

- Ladybugs – great for killing off aphids.
- Lacewings – also good at eating aphids, whitefly, and thrips.
- Praying Mantis – these will take care of beetles, caterpillars, leafhoppers, and whitefly.
- Spider Mite Predators – these kill spider mites.

We will talk about pest control in the chapter 'pests.'

Premade aquaponics systems
Don't spend money on premade systems. They are costly, and you won't have the fun of creating one yourself. Creating one yourself allows you to learn new things and provides a solid knowledge base in case you want to expand in the future.

Patience
One extra thing you will need to get your system started is a little patience.

It takes time for bacteria to appear and start multiplying. Therefore, your system can take as long as 6 weeks to become established before the nitrification works optimally.

As eager as you are to get started, you will need to have plenty of patience before you can start seeing the fruits of your labor. Patience can be the hardest part of the entire process!

Budget

There is a big difference between the cost of a small system and a full-scale commercial system. It is worth considering what size system you would like to construct and calculate an estimate of the costs involved in buying the initial equipment and looking after the fish and plants (don't forget the fish feed).

You can keep costs low by creating some components like the biofilter and solids filter yourself.

Once you have all these components, you will be ready to start building your system and producing your own fish and plants!

Let's look at some of the benefits and the impact aquaponics has on the environment.

The Benefits of Aquaponics

You probably don't need much convincing to believe that aquaponics is a better system for the environment. It can produce more food at a faster rate than traditional farming with a fraction of the water.

But these are not the only benefits. In fact, they are simply the biggest benefits to commercial farmers. Here are some more benefits when you use aquaponics:

Reduced disease
One of the biggest threats to most plants is the pests that live in the soil. They can attack the roots or simply deprive them of the nutrients they need. they can even cause death to one plant or kill a huge number of plants in one fell swoop. That's why agriculture uses pesticides to prevent it.

There is much less risk of this happening in an aquaponics system. There is no soil and, therefore, no soil-based pests. There are still pests in an aquaponics system, but significantly less than there are in soil-based production.

Less growing space
Because the roots are in the growing media or water which have direct access to all the nutrients, there is no competition between the different plants for nutrition.

The result is that plants can be much closer to each other than in traditional farming methods. Done properly, you can, therefore, produce more plants per square foot than traditional soil farming.

This is what allows you to create a small but productive aquaponics system in your backyard or wherever you like!

Provides two sources of food

Considering this type of farming can provide an increased yield compared to traditional methods, a further bonus is the fact that you can get two food sources from one system. As the plants grow and flourish, you will be able to harvest the fish and eat them.

Continuous production

As you become more familiar with aquaponics, you may adapt your system and have plants in various stages of growth. Essentially, you can create a continuous supply of food by having several grow beds and starting your plants in succession, creating a never-ending harvest. Yes, you can do this too with traditional farming, but with aquaponics, it is much easier.

Nelson and Pade greenhouse using continuous production

It is basically planting a new set of lettuce every week. With DWC, you can push the rafts further. You can leave space at both ends of your DWC system. One end for the seeding area and the other end for the harvesting area. The lettuce will travel from the seeding area and mature until it reaches the harvest area.

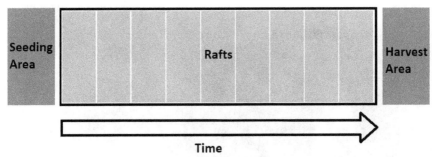

An efficient continuous production DWC setup

Faster growing rates
Once your system is set up, and the cycling is done, aquaponic systems are faster at producing fresh vegetables than soil-based growing.

No weeding
Because there is no soil in this type of growing system, you will not suffer from weeds. As a result, you will spend a lot less time weeding. You can spend that saved time looking after your system instead and making sure the plants grow as healthy as possible.

Grow almost anything
Aquaponics does not restrict your ability to grow the produce you want. Any plant can flourish in this type of system as they are still being given the nutrients, light, and water they need.

I have seen grow beds with trees in them! I would only advise this if you have an established system and have a few nitrates to spare. A ¾ inch river rock media is preferred because it can hold down the heavy tree.

Murray Hallam was growing a papaya fruit tree in aquaponics.

No need to water
Aquaponics means that there is water flowing to the plants all the time. This gives them all the water they need. You don't need to concern yourself with watering schedules. You need to top up the water level occasionally because the plants use the water, and it will evaporate. You can use an automatic top-up system that uses a float switch.

These are many of the reasons why aquaponics is so successful and growing in popularity; you can grow almost anything with very little effort.

Sustainability
The fact that you use less water and can produce more plants in less space and less time makes an aquaponics system a viable option.

The system is practically self-sustaining. Your main role will be to:

- Monitor the temperature and pH
- Feed the fish
- Drain the solids filter(s)
- Harvest produce and fish

Environmental Impact

Aquaponics is a viable option for the provision of food in the modern world where land and resources are becoming increasingly scarce. This is especially true in the developed world where land is needed for residential purposes.

Alongside this, there is an increase in consumer demand for fish, which cannot be supported by traditional fish farms. Unfortunately, this method of producing fish results in the release of toxic chemicals into the water at high quantities.

If you search for the following documentary on YouTube, you will have an idea about the problem we are facing.

'Farmed Norwegian Salmon World's Most Toxic Food'
Or here: https://www.howtoaquaponic.com/toxic-fish

But that is not the only issue with traditional farming methods. You may be surprised to learn that it can take 13 gallons of water to produce one lettuce in a soil-grown environment.

Using aquaponics, the same lettuce can be produced with 1.3 gallons of water; that's just 10% of the original water input!

In addition, aquaponics uses approximately ¼ of the space that traditional farming methods use to produce the same amount of food. The controlled environment of aquaponics can also help to ensure that crops grow faster. In fact, they can reach maturity in a little more than half the time of a traditional method (4-6 weeks in aquaponics for lettuce).

It is also important to consider the effects of pesticides that are commonly used in traditional farming methods.

These pesticides will help the crops get rid of pests. They also soak through into the soil and eventually end up in the rivers, the water supply and the food you are eating. These fertilizers can genetically modify, or even worse, kill other animals.

Pesticides are filtered out at a water treatment plant, but it still could end up in the groundwater.

This isn't an option when using aquaponics; any chemical pesticide would kill the fish and bacteria in the system. Not only is aquaponics a better option for the environment, it is also an excellent system to ensure that you can't cheat. The plants are completely organic.

The environmental benefits are clear, but this is not the only thing you need to be aware of when choosing an aquaponics system.

You can decide to have the installation inside a greenhouse, which will protect your crops from any fertilizers and pesticides which are sprayed nearby, so the wind cannot carry them onto your plants.

It is also much easier to manage the temperature and other variables when you are growing in an enclosed space. It also means that you can keep growing throughout the year, no matter how the weather is outside.

It is also interesting to note that an aquaponic system can be created virtually anywhere. In effect, you can make the food where it is needed, effectively reducing the 'gas miles;' and the amount of pollution that is being put into the atmosphere.

Let's dive deeper into the technology that makes aquaponics special.

Biological Surface Area

What is BSA?

You may not have heard or thought about the importance of the biological surface area in aquaponics, but it is a key factor in the success or failure of your system.

In short, the biological surface area is the amount of surface area available for your bacteria to live on. These bacteria are absolutely essential for the conversion of ammonia and ammonium to nitrites and then nitrates, and, therefore, a healthy aquaponics system. The greater the surface area, the more bacteria your system can support, and consequently, the more food you can grow and fish you can stock.

Having more bacteria means less toxic ammonia and more nitrates, which will be beneficial to plant life in your system.

So, if I have enough surface area, I'm all good?
This is not entirely true.

It is possible for a small setup to beat a bigger one. Why? Because bacteria require oxygen to transform ammonia to nitrites and then to nitrates. If the big setup doesn't have any oxygen in it and the small one does, the small one wins.

The point I am trying to make is that your bacteria need oxygen. Aim for at least 5ppm in your system.

- In a growbed, you create oxygen by flood and drain setups and an air stone in your fish tank.

- In NFT, you supply oxygen with air stones in your fish tank and biofilter.
- In a DWC system, you supply oxygen in your fish tank, in your biofilter, under your floating rafts, and in a degasser (if you need one).

Now you know what's important in your system. Let's talk some more about BSA.

The biological surface area (BSA) is measured by the number of square feet (ft^2) in your system that bacteria can live on. Imagine a square box that is 1 cubic foot. If you fill the box entirely with water, you will have 6 feet of BSA because there is $6ft^2$ of surface area the bacteria can live on.

We could greatly increase the BSA if we put some bio-media like rocks in the box, creating more surface area.

Calculating the BSA

For growbeds:

There are two kinds of biological surfaces you can calculate.

- System BSA.
- Media BSA.

Total BSA = system BSA + media BSA

System BSA: the total surface area of your system (fish tanks, piping, floating rafts, liners, etc.)

Media BSA: the total amount of surface area of your media in your grow beds or biofilter.

System BSA
If you want, you can calculate the BSA of your whole system. It would be a waste of time when working with a small DIY grow bed system.

It will be of more practical use if you calculate the BSA of a commercial floating raft setup because it has a lot more surface area (the underside of the rafts, the pond liner, tanks, etc.).

Media BSA
Most of your BSA will come from your grow media or bio media. That is what I am going to discuss next.

To calculate the media BSA, you will need to know what your Specific Surface Area (SSA) of your media is. This is effectively the measurement in square feet of the media. The unit of SSA is square feet per cubic feet (ft^2/ft^3).

For example, take a handful of river rocks. You need to calculate the specific surface area of these rocks (SSA). To calculate this, you could measure every single piece of rock. This will give you the surface area of each individual rock.

Add all the rocks together, and you will have the total surface area of the rocks in your hand.

Of course, you don't want to measure every piece of rock in your aquaponics system!

That is why there are standard values. These will give you a guide for the SSA of different growing media.

For a grow bed:

- Sand – 270 ft²/ft³
- ¾ inch crushed granite – 45-60 ft²/ft³
- Expanded clay (hydroton) – 70 ft²/ft³
- Lava rock – 85 ft²/ft³
- Pea gravel – 85 ft²/ft³
- River rock – 20 ft²/ft³

Sand has an SSA of 270 ft²/ft³. That's perfect, isn't it?
Not really, while sand has a huge SSA, it is not good because it will retain solids passing through it, resulting in anaerobic zones in no time if done incorrectly.

However, there are some systems that use sand as a growing media. It is called sandponics. In this book, I will not talk about sandponics because I don't have experience with this system, and few people use it.

Pea gravel is not the best choice either. Because of its close-packed makeup, solids are bound to be trapped, at the top making a stinky mess.

Do not use coco coir or any other organic matter as your bio media. It will decompose over time.

Example:
In our previous example of the cut and flip IBC, we know that the submerged media-filled bed is 48 inches by 48 inches and 12 inches deep.

The total height of the grow media will be 13 inches, but only 12 inches is submerged in water. If we calculate the volume, we get:

$$48x48x12 = 27,648 \ inches^3$$

Convert cubic inches to cubic feet:

$$\frac{27648 \ inches^3}{1728} = 16ft^3$$

16 cubic feet for the volume of one 48"x48"x12" grow bed.

BSA = Volume of grow bed x SSA

I would like to fill the media bed with expanded clay (hydroton). I look at the bullet-pointed list from before and see it has an SSA of 70 ft²/ft³.

$$16ft^3 x \ 70\frac{ft^2}{ft^3} = 1120 \ ft^2$$

We have a result **1120 ft²** for the entire grow bed.

We need 50ft² BSA per pound of fish to get rid of the toxic ammonia. If we then calculate how many fish I want, we use the following formula:

$$Fish = \frac{BSA}{50ft^2}$$

$$Fish = \frac{1120ft^2}{50ft^2} = 22 \ fish$$

You will need to give some room for these fish. A rate of 2-4 gallons per pound of fish is considered ideal for tilapia. If tilapia gets stocked at lower rates, they become territorial and aggressive to each other. This fish density depends on the fish you are trying to grow.

$$22 \ fish \ x \ 2 \ gallons = 44 \ gallons$$

I need a tank of at least 44 gallons to house 22 fish with a 16ft^3 hydroton filled growbed.

If we would repeat the same calculation with ¾ inch gravel, we could only stock 14 fish.

For DWC, NFT, and vertical towers

With the grow beds, your bacteria have enough space to create colonies because of the surface area of the hydroton or other media. With a high-density DWC or NFT system, there is no grow media for the bacteria to colonize. They can only colonize the system's total surface; that's about it.

Depending on your total BSA, you need additional filtration. This is called a biofilter.

With low-density DWC systems (0.3), you don't need one because the system BSA will take care of the limited fish waste.

With high densities DWC systems (1.5), you will most likely need a biofilter because the system BSA is not enough to get rid of the toxic ammonia and nitrites. More information about low and high density later in the book.

A biofilter doesn't use hydroton or river rock. It uses special fabricated media, which is used for pond filtration. This media is more expensive than natural media like river rock. You probably need to buy it online or from a pond store.

Here are some common BSA values:

For a biofilter:

- Bio tube media – 125 ft²/ft³
- White Matala filter media – 171 ft²/ft³
- Blue Matala filter media – 124 ft²/ft³
- Kaldnes (K1) – 250 ft²/ft³

For vertical growing towers:

- Zip grow matrix media – 290 ft²/ft³

Remember the following formula from the previous chapter?

$$Total\ BSA = System\ BSA + Media\ BSA$$

It applies to every BSA calculation. We are going to calculate the system BSA first and then the media BSA.

Before moving on to explaining biofilters, I want to give you an example setup of a small DIY non-commercial DWC system with a biofilter.

System BSA
The DIY non-commercial DWC system has a length of 10 feet, 5 feet wide, and 1 foot high (submersed area). It has a total growing area of 50ft² and a total surface area of 130ft².

$$2x\ (LxW) + (LxH) + (WxH)$$
$$2x\ (10x5) + (10x1) + (5x1) = 130ft²$$

The root area of lettuce is 10ft²/ft² (average in a continuous production facility).

This creates a surface area for the roots:

$$10\frac{ft^2}{ft^2} \; x \; 50ft^2 = 500ft^2$$

Now we add the surface area and the root area together.

$$130ft^2 + 500ft^2 = 630ft^2$$

Using the system's BSA alone, we could stock only 12 one-pound fish.

Media BSA
I install a biofilter with the media K1 (Kaldnes). It has an SSA of 250ft²/ft³.

I opt for a moving bed biofilter and build it in a 55-gallon drum with an air stone on the bottom to provide oxygen to the bacteria.

I fill the biofilter with 3 cubic feet of the media K1. That's equal to 22.4 gallons of volume, which will perfectly fit in the 55-gallon drum.

$$3ft^3 \; x \; 250\frac{ft^2}{ft^3} = 750ft^2$$

750ft² of BSA for the K1 kaldnes media.

Total BSA
To get to know the total BSA, I add the system BSA and the media BSA together.

$$Total \; BSA = 630ft^2 + 750ft^2 = 1380ft^2$$

1380ft² of total system BSA.

How many fish can I stock?

$$Fish = \frac{BSA}{50ft^2}$$

$$\frac{1380ft^2}{50ft^2} = 27 \; pounds \; of \; fish$$

50ft² is a static value referring to how much surface area is needed to convert all the toxic ammonia from one pound of fish.

The optimal ratio to convert fish food to all the available nutrients is 60 to 100 grams/m² per day in high-density DWC. Now we need to calculate if this amount of fish can eat 60 – 100 grams/m²/day.

We have a growing area of 50ft². If we convert that to m², we need to divide by 10.764.

$$\frac{50ft^2}{10.764} = 4.645m^2$$

Because we will have 27 fish in the system at one pound each, we need to feed the fish the following amount:
If we feed on the lower end:

$$4.645m^2 \; x \; 60 \; grams = 278 \; grams \; of \; feed \; per \; day$$

If we feed more:

$$4.645m^2 x \; 100 \; grams = 464.5 \; grams \; of \; feed \; per \; day$$

Tilapia eats 5 grams per day each day (average) to reach one pound in 6 months (more about this calculation later in the book).

$$27 \text{ } fish \text{ } x \text{ } 5 \text{ } grams = 135 \text{ } grams \text{ } of \text{ } feed \text{ } per \text{ } day$$

How much feed per square meter?

$$\frac{135 grams}{4.645 m^2} = 29 grams \text{ } per \text{ } m^2 per \text{ } day$$

You notice that we are way lower than the recommended feeding ratio of 60-100grams/m²/day. This result will be good for low-density systems with a combination of mineralization. System density is:

$$\frac{27 \text{ } pounds \text{ } of \text{ } fish}{50 ft^2 of \text{ } grow \text{ } area} = 0.54$$

These calculations can be a bit overwhelming, but I will explain them further in the book. If you want to grow more fish and have all nutrients readily available in your system without the need for mineralization, you need to increase the amount of feed.

You will need to increase the amount of fish in the system in order to put in more food. More food equals more nutrients for the plants. But more food means more waste (ammonia) that needs to be processed in the system.

If you add another two of those biological filters with K1 that has a surface area of 750ft², you can increase the fish stocking density.

We become a new total BSA of:

$$630 ft^2 + 750 ft^2 + 750 ft^2 + 750 ft^2 = 2880 ft^2$$

How many fish can I stock?

$$Fish = \frac{BSA}{50ft^2}$$

$$\frac{2880ft^2}{50ft^2} = 57.6 \; pounds \; of \; fish$$

If we calculate the feed required for 57.6 pounds of fish which eat an average of 5 grams a day we become:

$$57.6 \; x \; 5 \; grams = 288 \; grams \; of \; feed \; per \; day$$

This is in between the recommended minimum requirements for running a high-density aquaponics system.

How much feed per square meter?

$$\frac{288 grams}{4.645m^2} = 62 \; grams \; per \; m^2 per \; day$$

System density is:

$$\frac{57.6 \; pounds \; of \; fish}{50ft^2 of \; grow \; area} = 1.15$$

How much water do you need?

$$57.6 \; pounds \; of \; fish \; x \; 2 = 116 \; gallons$$

Increasing and decreasing feed rate

If you are running low on nutrients, you can increase the feed while making sure you have enough biofiltration.

If you have too much ammonia or nitrites, you need to decrease the feed or increase biofiltration.

You cannot have too much biofiltration. Having too much biofiltration or bacteria will be beneficial.

We have calculated the biological surface area for the media bed and biological filter media. But what is a biological filter? Read about it in the next chapter.

Biological filters

Biofiltration is probably something you will have to use when you are using a high-density system. It will help remove the toxic ammonia that the fish create. If you run a low-density system, you generally don't need a biological filter.

To recap, you most likely need a biological filter if you run a high-density DWC, NFT, or vertical system. If you use a grow bed, you generally don't need a biofilter unless you have too much fish for the BSA of your growbed.

The DIY biofilters are mostly made of 55-gallon plastic drums. We are going to fill them with filter media people use in koi ponds. They are more effective for standalone filters because they have more surface area than rocks or expanded clay.

The water comes through the solids lifting overflow to the solids removal filter or separator. Then it enters the biofilter and then moves on to the DWC, NFT, or any other system.

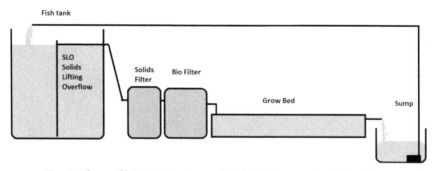

Typical small DWC setup with biofilter and solids filter

There are three types of biofilters for aquaponics:

- The fixed bed filter.
- The moving bed biofilm reactor.
- The trickle filter.

It is important to note that you should not clean the media inside of your biofilter. You will remove the bacteria and basically start with a new system.

Fixed bed filter

The fixed bed filter, also called a static bed filter, is 'static' when the biological surface doesn't move. In other words, the biological media, where the bacteria live, just sits in a container. This can be achieved with any material that has a high surface area like Matala filter media.

Matala Bio media mats

Each color has its own density and different SSA. Don't bother with the black and green ones because the surface area is too small. Either go with the blue or the grey one.

You can lay it down in the filter, but don't forget to put an air stone at the bottom. It's best to let the water come in from the top, and the outlet should be at the bottom.

Why?
Because there may be some solids left, you could catch them by using a mesh that covers the whole top of the drum. The mesh will also act as denitrification. You need to wash this mesh often to remove trapped solids. More on denitrification later.

This is an example of a fixed bed biofilter:

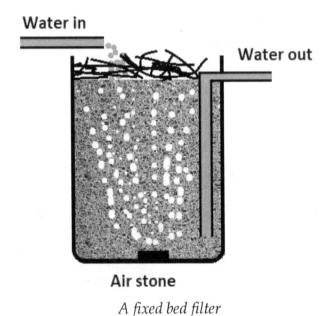

A fixed bed filter

Moving bed biofilm reactor (MBBR)

This is my preferred type of biofilter. It is also a 55-gallon drum that is filled with water, and you put K1 kaldnes in it (60% filling). On the bottom, there is an air stone that 'lifts' up and circulates the small K1 bio media.

Adding 3ft³ of K1 will give you a BSA of 750ft² for one filter. Size your air pump, so it equals one liter of air pumped to one liter of bio-media.

This way, you create a moving bed of bio media. This can be beneficial because you don't have rotting solids in your filter. The movement gets rid of dead bacteria populating the bio media. Just like the other filters, you can have several in a series or parallel to create the BSA you want for your system. It's best to buy bio-media in bulk from eBay or a nearby pond store.

Example of K1 Bio media

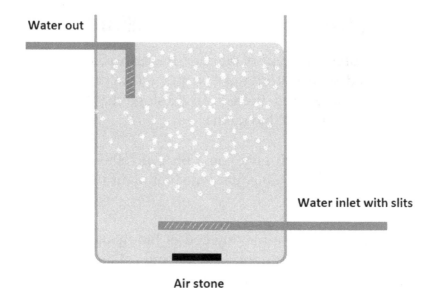

Water out

Water inlet with slits

Air stone

A moving bed biofilter

You will need to install a little filter cap on your incoming and exiting pipes to prevent the bio media from going through your system. You can do this by having pipes with slits in them.

A look at the surface of an MBBR

Drip filter

A drip filter does exactly what its name implies. It drips on your filter media, so your bacteria get lots of oxygen. You can compare it to a fixed bed filter but with a trickle on the media instead of submerged media.

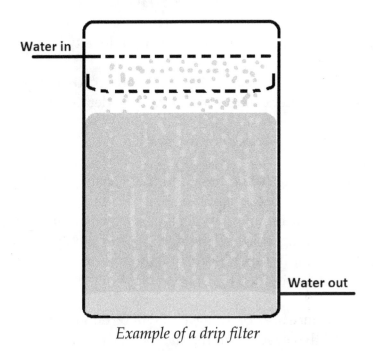

Water in

Water out

Example of a drip filter

I don't like the drip filter because not all your media will have bacteria on it. The water will take the easiest route down and will not go through all the media you have. Even if you do your best to distribute the water, it's not very effective. Which will, in turn, waste valuable bio media.

Now we know what biofilters are. You probably don't need one when you are using a media bed. If you do commercial aquaponics or large-scale backyard aquaponics, it is best to use biological filters. The next chapter will look at the difference between low- and high-density systems.

High Density vs. Low Density

When it comes down to commercial DWC fish stocking rates, there are two options. These are:

- Low-density DWC systems (LD) with a density of 0.3.
- High-density DWC systems (HD) with a density of 1.5.

For growbed systems, the recommended density is below one.

Each of these systems has its own advantages and disadvantages. Let's look at them in more detail:

Low-density deep-water culture system

If you are looking for an easy and inexpensive system, this is the one to go for. Because of the lower density, you don't need additional biofiltration. Low-density systems are used in areas where the selling price of the fish doesn't justify the cost of raising the fish. In other words: when you do not profit from selling the fish, you need to choose a low-density system.

The total surface area of the system will be enough to house the bacteria. In this system, ammonia and nitrite are zero most of the time. Nitrate is very close to zero (1 to 5ppm) but still enough to provide enough nitrogen (nitrate) to the plants.

A low-density system balances the nitrate levels close to zero. This means that you limit the fish food, thus decreasing the stocking density. With a low stocking density, you don't feed the fish the recommended 60-100grams/m² in a DWC culture system. Instead, you feed less to keep the nitrates close to zero.

When you use a low-density system without mineralization, you need additional supplementation of nutrients like phosphorous, potassium, calcium, and several others. You are basically running a normal hydroponics system.

That is why you need to install a mineralization tank to make sure every nutrient you put in the system (from the fish food) is used to feed your plants.

A system is considered low density when you divide the amount of fish (in pounds) in your system with the available growing area.
A low density is 0.3 pounds of fish per square feet of raft area.

$$Density = \frac{Fish\ in\ pounds}{Grow\ area\ in\ ft^2}$$

If you want to know how many pounds of fish you can stock with 1000ft² of growing area you apply the following formula:

$$Fish = Density\ x\ Grow\ area$$

$$0.3\ x\ 1000ft^2 = 300\ pounds\ of\ fish$$

The BSA of the system is, in most cases, enough to support the nitrifying bacteria. No additional biofiltration is generally needed. A mineralization tank is highly recommended to avoid nutrient deficiencies. Calculating the biological surface area is still necessary to be safe.

High-density deep-water culture system

If you are able to make money off the fish harvest, then this system makes more sense from an economic standpoint. The disadvantage with this system is that you need biofiltration, denitrification, and more solids filtration to get rid of the fish waste. This is a higher investment but can pay off in the long run.

I will talk more about denitrification in the advanced techniques chapter.

A system is considered high density if you have 1.5 pounds of fish/square feet of raft area.

$$Density = \frac{Fish \ in \ pounds}{Grow \ area \ in \ ft^2}$$

If you want to know how many pounds of fish you can stock with 1000ft² of growing area, you apply the following formula:

$$Fish = Density \ x \ Grow \ area$$

$$1.5 \ x \ 1000 ft^2 = 1500 \ pounds \ of \ fish$$

Growbed density

In hobby growbed systems, the biofiltration, solids breakdown, and mineralization will occur in your growbeds. You generally don't need to add additional solids filtration or biofiltration if you size your system correctly.

$$Density \ of \ growbeds = 1$$

A growbed system doesn't need additional solids filtration if you use a density of 1 or less. If you use this density, the amount of grow media is enough to break down the solids. The grow area always needs to be 12 inches deep (standard).

For example, an IBC system with 3 growbeds from cut IBC's and one IBC as a fish tank will have a total grow area of 36ft² ($3x12ft^2$). This system is called the 'advanced IBC setup' in the 'system designs' chapter at the end of the book.

This is how many fish you can stock:

$$\frac{36ft^2}{1} = 36\ pound\ of\ fish$$

Your growbeds will be able to handle the solids waste of 36 pounds of adult fish if you feed the recommended feeding ratio, which I will talk about in the 'feeding rates' chapter.

$$Growbed\ density = \frac{Fish\ in\ pounds}{Growing\ area\ in\ ft^2 with\ 12"\ depth}$$

$$Fish = Gowbed\ density\ x\ Growing\ area\ in\ ft^2 with\ 12"\ depth$$

$$Growing\ area\ in\ ft^2 with\ 12"\ depth = \frac{Fish\ in\ pounds}{Density}$$

We have learned that there are different densities for every system. Keep these numbers in mind if you are sizing your aquaponics system. They could save you a lot of money if you do commercial aquaponics.

Fish Stocking

Now we have arrived at the fun part. The primary section that makes aquaponics stand out from the rest. In this chapter, I am going to explain the math that is involved in aquaponics. You might want to read this a few times over to really understand it.

Fish stocking density, feeding rates, and plant density are all calculated using math. There is no guessing. If you are not willing to do this first, you will be understocking and have nutrient deficiencies.

You can calculate this in two ways:

- How many fish do I want?
- How much growing space do I want?

You need to calculate the growing space first because it will be the most profitable and, most of the time, your limiting factor because of available space. The best way of explaining this is to use an example. I am going to reverse engineer the famous UVI system (resource mentioned in notes).

They have 6 floating raft beds for a total growing area of 214m² (2300ft²). We are going to calculate how many fish they can stock so all the fish waste is converted to nutrients.

How much feed input do I need to supply a growing area of 214m² with nutrients? A proven amount is 60 to 100 grams of feed per square meter of growing area in a DWC system. In this example, we will take 80 grams of feed per square meter.

If we take the 214m² and calculate the total amount of feed we need in order to supply the nutrients to the plants, we have:

$$214m^2 x\ 0.08kg = 17.12kg$$

17.12kg of feed to supply 214m² of growing area in a day.

Now we need to calculate how many fish we need to consume 17.12kg of fish food in one day. This depends on the kind of fish and if it's a small fish or mature fish. One pound of small fish will need more feed than one pound of mature fish. You need to keep in mind that the fish will grow, so one pound of fingerlings will become many pounds of adult fish.

If we take tilapia, we can see that the feeding rate depends on the growth rate. If we stock all our fish at the same time, they will all be mature at the same time, which will result in a big fluctuation of nutrients to the plants.

Tilapia Growth and Feeding Rates

Month	Start Weight (g)	End Weight (g)	Growth Rate g/day	Feeding Rate (% weight)
1	1	5	0.2	15 - 10
2	5	20	0.5	10 - 7
3	20	50	1.0	7 - 4
4	50	100	1.5	4 - 3.5
5	100	165	2.0	3.5 - 2.5
6	165	250	2.5	2.5 - 1.5
7	250	350	3.0	1.5 - 1.25
8	350	475	4.0	1.25 - 1.0
9	475	625	5.0	1.0

Growth and feeding rate for tilapia

Instead, they opt for four different tanks where fish are dropped in at different growing stages. This will equalize the nutrients that are produced. You would have one tank with new fingerlings (2 months old), one with 4-month old fish, one with 6-month old fish, and the last one with 8-month old fish. Each will get an appropriate feeding rate for their size. And will be harvested every 6 months.

If we decided to raise tilapia and buy them as fingerlings when they are around 2 months old, it would take 6 months to raise the fish to plate size, which is 450 grams (1 pound).

In one year, the fish would consume:

$$17.12 kg \ of \ fish \ feed \ x \ 365 \ days = 6,248.8 kg$$

Divide this by the feed conversion rate:

$$\frac{6,248.8 kg}{2} = 3,124 \ kg \ of \ fish \ weight \ gain \ in \ one \ year$$

Convert kilograms to pounds:

$$3,124 \ x \ 2.205 = 6,889 \ pounds \ of \ fish \ gain \ in \ one \ year$$

Divide this by the weight of the fish by harvest:

$$\frac{6,889}{1 \ pound} = 6,889 \ fish \ harvested \ in \ one \ year$$

One year is twelve months. Time to harvest is 6 months. This means we can harvest a fish tank two times each year

There are 4 fish tanks in this system.

It takes 6 months or 182 days before harvesting.

$$\frac{182 \ days}{4 \ tanks} = 45.5 \ days \ between \ harvests$$

$$\frac{365 \ days \ in \ one \ year}{45.5 \ days \ between \ harvests} = 8 \ harvests \ a \ year$$

The feed conversion rate (FCR) for tilapia is 2. This means it will take 2 pounds (900 grams) of fish feed to raise a one-pound fish (450 grams).

There are 182 days in 6 months. If we divide the 900 grams of feed by 182, we know the average amount of feed we need in one day for one fish.

$$\frac{900 \ grams}{182} = 5 \ grams \ of \ fish \ feed \ per \ day$$

The food we put in the system each day is 17.12kg. We need to divide this weight with the weight of food a fish consumes daily.

$$\frac{17.12kg}{0.005kg} = 3424 \ pounds \ of \ fish$$

3424 fish divided over 4 tanks, that's around 856 fish in a tank.

Low or high density?

$$Density = \frac{Fish \ in \ pounds}{Grow \ area \ in \ ft^2}$$

$$\frac{3424 \ pounds \ of \ fish}{2300ft^2} = 1.49$$

1.49 is a high-density system.

Now we need to calculate how big of a fish tank we need to house the fish. The UVI (University of the Virgin Islands) uses a stocking density for tilapia at 3.43 gallons per pound of fish. If we use this ratio, we will get:

$$856 \; fish \; x \; 3.43 \; gallons = 2,936 \; gallons$$

We need a 3000-gallon fish tank to house 856 tilapia or an 11.3m³ tank. We need 4 of these to house all the 3424 fish.

A total of 3424 fish will eat all the food that is required to have no nutrient deficiencies in the system if you are feeding at the specified rate and discharge the settable solids (more on this later).

The average feeding rate of 5 grams a day will produce the most efficient growth of your fish. If you don't make money on the fish, there will be other options available, which I will talk about next.

Why would you use more than one tank?

- More but smaller tanks could be cheaper.
- More control over the fish.
- Grow more than 4 batches in a 6-month period.
- Grow other fish species.

That's it! That's how you calculate fish stocking. But now we need to look at some other very important factors.

Let's look a bit more at high density versus low density for commercial systems. We have talked about low and high density briefly in the previous chapter.

You must be thinking; I'm going to make a lot of money on these fish! But this is where the return on investment comes in (ROI).

You see, commercial aquaponics is a totally different game than backyard aquaponics. Your setup needs to be commercially viable. And sometimes, you are going to lose money on your fish (depends on local market prices).

First, we need to know the costs of raising one pound of tilapia. These are the factors that need to be considered:

- Fingerling price ($1.75).
- Food price (2 pounds).
- 3 kW/h of electricity (@$0.12/kWh).
- 0.11 hours of labor.

$$\$1.75 + (2x\$1) + (3x\$0.12) + (0.11x\$15) = \$5.76$$

The total price for fish is $5.76 per pound. But the market only buys for $3 per pound. That's a loss of $2.76 per fish!

Yes, if the numbers don't favor you, you are in trouble!

Well, not entirely.

The system we calculated in the previous example was the UVI (University of the Virgin Islands) system. They grow as much fish as they can because fish are profitable. We call such a system a high-density system (HD). There are as many fish as physically possible. A high-density system requires biofiltration and solids separators, as we have previously discussed.

If we calculate the density of a high-density system, we will be in the range of 1.5. If we calculate it for the UVI system, it will be:

$$\frac{3424 \; pound \; of \; fish}{2300 ft^2} = 1.49$$

If I am going to lose money on fish, do I need to stock that many fish in my system?

No.

The founders of friendlyaquaponics.com, Tim Mann, and Susanne Friend worked with the UVI system as well. They lost thousands of dollars on the fish in their first year of operating. This was because local market prices were not favorable.

They decided to cut back on the amount of fish. They now run their aquaponic systems at a rate of 0.3 pounds of fish per ft² of growing area. They run their water straight from the fish tank to the DWC system without problems. They don't have filtration or biofilters. All the filtering is done naturally because the small number of fish will produce less waste.

If we calculate how many fish we would need in the UVI system for a 0.3 ratio, and we know our grow area, then we know the amount of fish we need.

$$Fish \; in \; pounds = Density \; x \; Grow \; area$$

$$0.3 \; x \; 2300 ft^2 = 690 \; pounds \; of \; fish$$

Running an aquaponics system at a low density is called Low-Density systems or LD. Here are the benefits of a LD system:

- Generally, no biofiltration is needed
- Less complex
- If the price of fish is low, you don't lose as much money on fish.

I recommend you use solids removal and a mineralization tank in a commercial LD system.

The reason for this is simple: there still will be solids in the system which will settle in the DWC troughs. They will mineralize in these troughs, but a layer of solids waste will start to create anaerobic zones (zones without oxygen). This will limit the biological surface area of your system.

What density is right for you?

In commercial systems, it all depends on your local price to raise a pound of fish, and the price the market is willing to pay. The fish cost calculation is a good example to compare with. Check your local fish prices and see how much you will get for a pound of fresh organic fish.

- If the calculation is positive, it's a wise choice to go for a high-density system.

- If the calculation is negative, it makes more sense to have a low-density system.

What about bacteria in a HD and LD system?

In a high-density system, you need more bacteria than a low-density system. Let's explore why:

$$BSA = \frac{50ft^2 x\ 0.46}{Pounds\ of\ fish}$$

HD BSA:

$$\frac{50ft^2 x\ 0.46}{3300\ fish} = 75,900ft^2 of\ BSA\ required$$

LD BSA:

$$\frac{50ft^2 x\ 0.46}{690\ fish} = 15,870ft^2 of\ BSA\ required$$

As a rule, you need 50 square feet of surface area (BSA) per pound of fish to convert the ammonia to nitrates.

Because in commercial systems, we use more than one fish tank, we have a mix of mature and young fish. The ratio of 50ft²/pound of fish drops down. On average, the fish will weigh 211 grams or 0.46 pounds (that's why I have added the 0.46).

The fish are introduced as 2-month old fingerlings.

Fish age	Fish weight	Time
2 months	20 grams	Entering the system
4 months	100 grams	2 months in the system
6 months	252 grams	4 months in the system
8 months	475 grams	6 months in the system

Calculate the average fish weight:

$$20\ grams + 100\ grams + 252\ grams + 475\ grams = 847\ grams$$

$$\frac{847\ grams}{4} = 211\ grams\ or\ 0.46\ pounds$$

You can see from the calculation that an HD system needs more surface area to convert ammonia to nitrates than an LD system. This is because there is more fish food that needs to be converted to usable nutrients.

Coming back to the example, let's calculate the total BSA of the 2300ft² system.
The growing area is 2300ft².
The BSA of the raft area is 10.000 ft².
The BSA of the piping and tanks is around 5.000ft².
The roots have a BSA of 23.000ft² (10ft²/ft²).

In total, we have:

$$10,000ft^2 + 5,000ft^2 + 23,000ft^2 = 38,000ft^2$$

The LD system is under the 38,000 ft² of available BSA. This means we do not need additional biofiltration.

But the HD system is well above the total available BSA!

HD systems operate at higher ammonia levels than LD systems. That's why HD systems have biofilters to increase their available BSA.

In the case of the UVI system, the remaining BSA is:

$$75,9000ft - 38,000ft^2 = 37,900ft^2$$

37,900ft² is supplied by the surface area of the clarifiers, filter tanks (biofilter), and degassing tank.

These HD systems operate at around 1-2ppm of ammonia, while LD systems run on 0 to 0.25ppm. You should note that tilapia is more tolerant of higher ammonia levels than other fish.

If your fish aren't profitable commercially, there is no reason why you shouldn't use a LD system. A LD system will still provide nutrients to the plants providing the nitrate levels are not zero and in combination with a mineralization tank. Regular checks for nutrients in the water should be made.

I do not recommend growing fruiting crops like tomatoes and peppers in a LD system because it will require more nutrients to grow.

> **If the fish are not making money you should operate in a way to keep the nitrate levels right above zero. Which is using a low-density system. Use a 0.3 density ratio.**

Feeding Rates

The one I'm talking about in this book is the rate that the UVI system used in their aquaponics system. The feeding rate of 60-100 grams per square meter per day is generally accepted as the only proven feeding ratio to maximize fish and vegetable production.

In other words, if you were to feed your fish 60 to 100 grams per square meter of growing area per day, you would only have to add iron, calcium, and potassium to the system. More on these three nutrients later in the book.

The recommended feeding rate for an NFT system is 25% of these ratios, meaning 15 to 25 grams per square meter per day.

The recommended feeding ratio for media beds is 15-40 grams per square meter per day.

If we look at where the nutrients (other than nitrogen) come from, it's in the fish food. The fish food gets eaten by the fish, and it exits the fish in the form of what we call 'solids.' The number of solids produced is the reason why you need to have solids separators or filters installed.

The way you get rid of these solids plays a major role in the nutrients that are available to your plants. In the UVI system, with the feeding rate of 60 to 100 grams per square meter per day, the solids that were captured in the clarifier were drained from the system.

Solids disposal in the UVI system

In these images, you can see that the solids were used as fertilizer in soil gardening. This means that the nutrients put in the system (the fish feed) were not fully transferred and processed by bacteria to be used in the system.

The ratio of solids removal by the clarifiers is estimated to be in the range from 50% to 70%. Only the settable solids will get removed using a clarifier. The other solids that were too light to settle will be trapped in the filtering tanks (bird netting). This is where the remaining of the fish food gets broken down by bacteria into nutrients for the system. When these filter tanks were almost full of solids, they would clean them. The other part of the non-settable solids would be removed from the system, which means less nutrients that are being dissolved into the water.

The cleaning of the netting in the UVI system

Again, removing the solids from the system without letting them fully break down leads to a waste of valuable and expensive fish food. It could have been used as plant nutrients in the aquaponics system.

To conclude, the solids in the UVI system were not entirely processed by bacteria, and most were removed from the system. It leads to the feed input being more than what was used in the system.

If you are trying to grow as many fish as possible, that's a good thing. But if fish costs you money, you want to minimize feed input but still have all the nutrients available for your plants. That's when the following feeding ratio comes into play.

The system did not have nutrient deficiencies because of the large amount of feed input. They ran several water tests to make sure the plants did not have any deficiencies. They could afford to remove the fish waste in order to maximize profit on the fish (high density).

Another person had a different approach of keeping as much solid fish waste recirculated in the system without removing (draining) them. This person is called Dr. Wilson Lennard. He did research on the optimal feeding ratio in an aquaponics system without getting rid of solids.

He used a technique called mineralization, where the solids can break down by bacteria in a separate tank. I will talk more about this technique in the next chapter.

The point he made was that you don't need as much feed input into an aquaponics system as long as you mineralize the solids the fish produce. Furthermore, he successfully ran trails for 3 and a half years to find this optimal feeding ratio.

The ratio he found was that feeding at a rate of 16 grams of fish feed per square meter per day made all nutrients available for the plants. This is 3.75 to 6.25 times less than the feeding ratio the UVI system used. This is only the case if all solids are allowed to break down in a mineralization tank. The 16 grams of feed was used for leafy greens. If you are growing fruiting crops such as tomatoes, you would need to use more feed.

Let's quickly calculate what the density will be if we feed at 16 grams per square meter per day in the UVI system. These are the known values:

- 16 grams of feed per square meter per day.
- 214 m² or 2300 ft² of plant area.
- Tilapia has a feed conversion rate of 2.

First, calculate the amount of fish feed needed in a day:

$$16 \: grams \: x \: 214m^2 = 3{,}424 \: grams \: of \: fish \: feed \: per \: day$$

Then, calculate the amount of fish feed needed in 6 months:

$$3{,}242 \: grams \: x \: 182 \: days = 623{,}168 \: grams \: for \: 6 \: months$$

Next, convert to pounds:

$$\frac{623{,}168 \: grams}{454} = 1{,}372 \: pounds \: of \: feed \: for \: 6 \: months$$

The feed conversion rate for tilapia is 2.

$$\frac{1{,}372 \: pounds \: of \: fish \: food}{2} = 686 \: pounds \: of \: fish \: weight \: gain$$

Calculate the system density:

$$\frac{686 \: pounds \: of \: fish \: weight \: gain}{2300 ft^2 growing \: area} = 0.298$$

The system density is 0.298.

This number should ring a bell. It's very close to the actual number of a low-density system, which is 0.3.

So why did the UVI system dispose of the valuable solids? Because they were running a high-density system with the focus on producing as many fish as possible. The fish needed the amount of feed input to grow quickly.

What does this mean for backyard aquaponics?
Most hobby systems use growbeds. Growbeds are a form of mineralization. The solids will break down in the growbed by using earthworms and a flood and drain cycle.

Some people's growbeds gets clogged up. They will clean out the growbeds to start over again with a new one. The nitrification bacteria will suffer from this, and you will also remove some solids, which is not what you want.

That's why you should design growbeds using a ratio of one square foot of growing media (12 inches deep) for every pound of fish as a general guideline. Aim for a system density ratio of 1.

Calculation of a chop and flip aquaponics system:

Hydroton with 12 inches of depth.
The surface area is 3.2ft by 3.2ft.

$$3.2ft \ x \ 3.2ft = 10.24ft^2$$

Calculate the amount of fish:

$$Pounds \ of \ fish = Density \ x \ Growing \ area \ with \ 12" \ of \ depth$$

$$1 \ x \ 10.24ft^2 = 10.24 \ pounds \ of \ fish$$

You can have 10.24 pounds of fish in your growbed system if you use a chop and flip IBC system that measures 3.2x3.2ft.

Mineralization

What is mineralization?
Bacteria colonize the fish waste and release the minerals (nutrients) that are inside of the fish waste. It will give you a nutrient-rich substance that you can re-introduce in your system.

If you don't do this, you won't be converting the fish feed 100% to nutrients. So, it's basically optimizing the fish feed you put in your system. In a low-density DWC, NFT, or vertical system, a mineralization tank is essential.

In a high-density system, you can still include a mineralization tank. It would be a waste to let these nutrients flow away into your garden or drain. It's not necessary, but I still recommend it, especially if you grow fruiting crops.

If you have a high stocking density in a grow bed setup (above 1), I still recommend using a solids filter first before letting it flow to the growbeds. Use a mineralization tank to process the solids that come from the solid's filter. The fine solids that will pass the main solids filter will get processed in the growbeds. I will make sure to include an example of this in the last chapter: 'system designs.'

If you drain the solids from your solids filter, you need to redirect it to another tank. A separate mineralization tank is used for this exact purpose.

Here is an example setup with a mineralization tank:

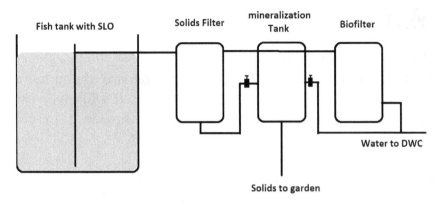

Setup with mineralization tank

The fish waste will get lifted with the SLO to the solids filter. The solids filter catches fish waste or uneaten food. The clean water from the solids filter goes directly to the biofilter. If you don't use a biofilter, it will go directly to the media beds.

Once in a while, when the solids build up in the solids filter, you need to flush them out. Before we open the left ball valve on the mineralization tank, we need to shut down the air pump inside the mineralization tank. We do this to allow the solids to settle to the bottom. Next, open the valve on the right side of the mineralization tank. Next, let half of the clean water from the mineralization tank drain to the DWC rafts or media beds.

Once the mineralization tank is drained halfway, we close the right valve and open the left valve. This will remove the solids from the solids filter and bring them to the mineralization tank through gravity. Once the mineralization tank is full, you close the left valve, and now the mineralization tank is isolated from the system. Now you need to power on the air pump so bacteria can continue to break down the new solids to usable minerals for the plants.

You may ask, what's the point of a solids filter when I will return the waste back to the system? Good question.

Indeed, the solids 'can' go to the rafts. But only if you're not careful. Remember the air stones we put in the system? They will bring all the solids up to the top of the tank and down again, like a moving bed biofilter. Once you decide to flush your solids filter, you need to turn off the air stones in the mineralization tank. You then wait a few minutes for the solids to settle before opening the ball valve to the right. This will ensure that no solids move from the mineralization tank back to your system. Additionally, you can use a filter sock on the outlet.

It's possible that not all your solids will break down. That's why there is an additional drain. Allow the solids to settle and then drain it. Just like you would do with a solids filter when you had no mineralization tank. Your plants in the garden will love this sludge.

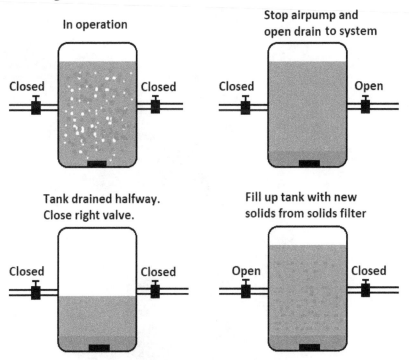

How a mineralization tank works

This is a system that works with gravity. You need to make sure you level your tanks correctly.

Step by Step Guide

By now, you should be getting excited! You have been enlightened as to what an aquaponic system is and how it can benefit the environment as well as creating an organic food source. You should also have an idea of all the basic equipment you need to get started on building your own system.

Of course, when you're first setting up, you're probably not thinking about creating enough food to feed the whole neighborhood. Succeeding in growing plants and keeping your fish healthy is a good starting point.

For this reason, you may want to start very small. However, I would caution against going too small; you'll simply create more work for yourself when you want to expand your setup. That's why it is good to follow this step by step guide. I recommend starting with a simple IBC setup.

Step 1 – Size

There are many reasons to start an aquaponics setup. You may want to grow enough food to feed your family, or you may prefer to start selling high-quality local produce at the market.

The point is that you need to decide what size yield you would like to achieve. Knowing how many plants you want to grow will allow you to work out the other details of your setup.

Your plants should be spaced according to the size you expect them to grow. For example, a lettuce head will need approximately 8 to 12 inches of growing space. The primary concern with plant spacing is to know which plants you are growing and how much room they need when they are ready for harvest.

Here is a general guideline that shows how many plants you can get per square foot:

- Basil – 4
- Carrots – 8
- Celery – 1
- Tomato – 1 per 4 square feet
- Lettuce leaf – 4
- Lettuce head – 1
- Onions – 4
- Spinach – 4

Lettuce spacing in a DWC system

Be warned that herbs like mint will spread quickly. It's best to keep an eye on these. Otherwise, they will take over your grow bed.

If you are growing the plant from seed, there will be a recommended spacing recommendation on the package of the seeds.

Once you've established the number of plants you want and the space they need, you'll have an idea regarding the size of the area you need to grow them (the growing pace).

Next, you need to decide what kind of system you are going to use. I recommend choosing the growbeds for your first system.

Growbeds are used for a hobby system, while floating rafts are used for commercial systems. I will continue with a growbed system because that what most people will use.

For example, an IBC container using the cut and flip technique (discussed at the beginning of this book) is 42 inches by 42 inches. That's a total area of 12.25 square feet. The image below are dimensions of common IBC's. In this example, I am using a 260-gallon IBC (1000liters).

STANDARD TANK SIZES			
CAPACITY (GALLONS)	BASE SIZES		OVERALL TANK HEIGHT
	A	B	C
180	36"	36"	40-1/2"
215	42"	42"	35"
250	42"	48"	35"
260	42"	42"	41"
300	42"	48"	41"
305	42"	42"	47"
350	42"	48"	47"
395	42"	42"	59"
450	42"	48"	59"
485	42"	42"	71"
550	42"	48"	71"

Dimensions of IBC totes

We learned from the plant spacing that one head of lettuce needs approximately 1ft².

We can plan our grow bed to have 4 squares by 4 squares. Totaling 16 squares of 0.76ft². This is in an IBC setup with one grow bed. Don't forget to include your siphon.

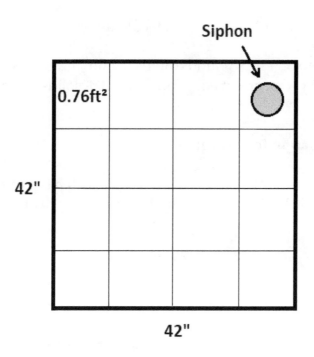

Grow bed spacing

The amount of fish will depend on your total grow area and your BSA. You need to follow the density ratio of 1 for growbeds if you want to get rid of all the solids using the growbeds.

If you have additional filtration installed, you can use the total BSA calculation. This setup will be more complicated, but you could stock more fish. We will start by calculating density first.

Density calculation:
One growbed of 3.5ft x 3.5ft has a total grow area of 12.25ft². It is filled with hydroton at a depth of 12 inches.

Using the density formula, we can stock 12 pounds of fish.

$$Fish\ in\ pounds = Density\ x\ grow\ area\ in\ ft^2$$

$$1 \times 12.25ft^2 = 12.25 \; pounds \; of \; fish$$

You can stock 12.25 pounds of fish, and the solids will be removed by the growbed. No additional solids filtration is needed.

BSA calculation for hydroton:

Using the same growbed of 3.5ft x 3.5ft, which has a total grow area of 12.25ft². It is filled with hydroton at a depth of 12 inches.

$$12.25ft^2 x \; 70 \; \frac{ft^2}{ft^3} = 857ft^2$$

The total BSA of the media is 857 ft².

To calculate how much fish this growbed can handle, you divide the BSA by 50ft².

$$\frac{857ft^2}{50ft^2} = 17 \; pounds \; of \; fish$$

Calculate the density:

$$\frac{17 \; pounds \; of \; fish}{12.25ft^2} = 1.38$$

The density is higher than the recommended density of one. Some additional solids and biofiltration is needed once the fish are reaching one pound. You can manipulate the density by reducing fish feed or harvesting some fish.

Using the ratio of 50ft² will only calculate the nitrification process. Not the disposal of fish waste.

BSA calculation for ¾ inch gravel:

$$12.25 ft^2 x\ 45 \frac{ft^2}{ft^3} = 454 ft^2$$

The total BSA of the media is 545 ft².

Amount of fish:

$$\frac{545\ ft^2}{50 ft^2} = 11\ pounds\ of\ fish$$

Calculate the density:

$$\frac{11\ pounds\ of\ fish}{12.25 ft^2} = 0.89$$

This is below the recommended density of one. You do not need additional solid filtration.

Note: Keep in mind that you cannot stock more than 11 pounds of fish if you use ¾ inch gravel. The total BSA is not enough to convert the fish waste to nitrates.

The total surface area of your grow media will make it possible to stock a lot of fish. But that isn't always good. Having more fish will lead to a decrease in growth. Read more on this when we decide the feed ratio for optimal growth.

50ft² is a static value referring to how much surface area is needed to convert all the toxic ammonia from one pound of fish to nutrients for the plants.

In the first example, we had a higher density than the growbed can handle. We can either:

A. Harvest some of the fish when they mature
B. Decrease initial stocking density

If we want to use the hydroton without any additional solids filtration (option B), we use the system ratio of 1.

$$1 \ x \ 12.25 ft^2 = 12.25 \ pounds \ of \ fish$$

You can have 12.25 pounds of fish if you use a growbed with hydroton without disposing of the solids.

To calculate the amount of water you need to house tilapia, you multiply the number of gallons per fish with the amount of fish your growbed can handle. The stocking density of Nile tilapia is one pound of fish for 2 to 3 gallons.

$$17 \ pounds \ of \ fish \ x \ 2 \ gallons = 34 \ gallons$$

Stocking density depends on which fish you are going to use. Tilapia is the fish with the highest stocking density. They are used to living in high stocking densities.

Rainbow trout, on the other hand, performs best at a stocking density of 1 pound per 8 gallons of water.

If you decide on stocking rainbow trout, you would need a tank that has:

$$17 \ pounds \ of \ fish \ x \ 8 \ gallons = \ 136 \ gallons$$

Feeding ratio
We have one growbed with a total growing area of 12.25ft². If we convert that to m², we need to divide by 10.764.

$$\frac{12.25 ft^2}{10.764} = 1.13 m^2$$

The recommended feeding ratio for growbeds is 15 to 40 grams per square meter per day.

If we feed on the lower end:

$$1.13m^2 x \; 15 \; grams = 17 \; grams \; of \; fish \; feed \; per \; day$$

If we feed more:

$$1.13m^2 x \; 40 \; grams = 45 \; grams \; of \; fish \; feed \; per \; day$$

Optimal growth
Having fewer fish in the system might be beneficial to the speed of growth for your fish. Fish will grow faster if they have to split 45 grams between 10 fish than they would when there are 20 fish.

If you feed ad libitum, which means feeding until they can't eat in a 5-minute window, you should consider adding solids filtration or expect to clean out your growbeds often if it's above the 40 grams ratio.

Another thing to consider is the optimal growth rate of the fish. In order to know the amount of feed a fish needs in a day for optimal growth, we can use some calculations:

- 1 tilapia is harvested at one pound (450 grams).
- It takes 6 months or 182 days for the tilapia to reach one pound.
- The feed conversion rate (FCR) of tilapia is 2.

$$450 \; grams \; x \; 2 = 900 \; grams \; of \; feed \; input$$

You need 900 grams of feed input to raise a one-pound tilapia.

$$\frac{900 \ grams}{182 \ days} = 5 \ grams \ of \ feed \ per \ day \ on \ average$$

If you feed each tilapia 5 grams per day (on average), they will reach one pound in 6 months if the conditions are ideal.

BSA or density ratio for growbeds?
We have calculated this system using BSA, and the ratio of fish/grow area (density).

BSA is mostly used to calculate DWC systems. The ratio of fish/grow area is used when using growbeds.

The reason for this is that if you calculate the fish stocking based on BSA, you will most likely have to install solid filters.

Calculating trough system density is much easier for hobby systems.

Step 2 – Growing Area

Once you've calculated how many fish you can have, you need to decide which type of system you are going to use.

If you're doing this for the first time, it's a good idea to start with a standard IBC grow bed. However, if you're feeling adventurous, you can opt for the deep-water culture that was discussed earlier in the book.

The standard media bed can be created from:

- IBC containers.
- 55-gallon drums cut lengthwise (barrelponics).
- Wood and liner.
- Concrete and liner.

- Plastic containers.
- Bathtubs.
- Plywood/cinderblocks and epoxy paint.

55-gallon drums cut lengthwise to make 'barrelponics.'

The DWC system is mostly created with wood and pond liner or concrete and food-grade epoxy paint. It should be at least 12 inches deep with air stones on the bottom. The width will depend on the material you will use as the rafts. The recommended material is medium to high-density Styrofoam that's not fire-retardant (because of chemicals) and 2 inches thick (50mm). You can spray or paint it white, so it reflects the sun. This way, it will not heat up your water. I talk about using paint in aquaponics later in the book.

If you are growing romaine lettuce, you need 2-inch net pots spaced about 8 inches center to center depending on the lettuce variety.

4 ft
48 inches
122 cm

8 ft
96 inches
244 cm

Plant spacing in a 4ft x 8ft DWC raft for lettuce

Standard 2 inch net cup

For the NFT system, you need a pipe with at least a diameter of 3 inches (7.6cm) and a decline of 4 degrees. The water in the NFT system needs to be very clean. If there are solids, they will attach themselves to the root of the plant and hinder the nutrient absorption of the plant and cause root rot, which is not good.

If you are using concrete or limestone, make sure it's not in contact with the water. It will increase the pH of your water, which the bacteria and plants do not like.

Step 3 – Location

Now you need to decide where you are going to grow. Part of this decision will be made by the size of your system. If it's small, you may want to set it up inside your home. If you do this, you'll need to make sure there is enough light for the plants to grow and flourish. This requires more electricity than growing outside. But because of the temperature inside, you may be able to grow it faster.

Larger setups will need to be outside to use the sun as a source of energy. Using lights will drive up the cost of production and will cut into your profits.

If your local weather is not consistent or likely to drop in temperature and damage your plants, you may need to consider building a greenhouse so you can grow year-round.

A greenhouse will make it much easier to monitor the environment and make sure the plants are getting all the sunlight they need.

Part of this decision will need to be related to the type of plants you are trying to grow; some flourish in cooler weather while others need the warmth and protection of a greenhouse.
A good choice is to use a greenhouse where you can roll up the sides to let in a breeze in the summer and close it in the winter. We will look at cooling and heating options later in the book.

Once you've decided where you want the setup to be, you need to create a plan. I advise drawing your setup first with all the pipework before you start doing anything.

Keep in mind that you want your design to be:

- As energy efficient as possible.
- A system that requires low maintenance.
- Adaptable for future upgrades.

After you have made the plan, you can start building.
You can put your grow beds and fish tank in the right position. Don't forget you will need power to run several parts of the system (pump, heater, fan, etc.). It is advisable to use a circuit that is designed to offer protection against water splashes and spills. This can prevent you or the fish from getting electrocuted!

Don't forget a large amount of water in a tank is going to be heavy. Consider installing a solid foundation before rainwater will erode the soil you have built your system on.

If you are growing indoors, then you want to make sure there will be no spills or at least make something to contain the water in if it spills.

Step 4 – Connecting It Up

Now you need to connect the grow bed and fish tank together. You'll need pipes to feed the water from the fish tank to the grow bed and another to take it back. It is also a good idea to have an overflow pipe set approximately an inch below the top of the growing media. This will help prevent an overflow if the siphon fails or is blocked.

If you're opting for a small system, you can place the grow bed on top of the tank and use gravity to allow the water to flow back into the fish tank.

You will need to add an aerator to add oxygen to the water, and your pump needs to be added to the fish tank.

The key is to have all the parts connected before adding the media. Once you've got the connections in place, you should test the system by adding water only and watch it cycle around the system. Pay attention to leaks; you don't want to be dealing with them once you added your grow media.

The Grow Media

As already mentioned, ¾ inch river rock or gravel is probably the cheapest option but not necessarily the most effective. However, you can choose any grow media that suits you providing it has a decent surface area. Hydroton is the most used media.

Whatever you decide to use, it should be pH neutral, and you should wash it before you add it to your grow beds. Your wet growing media should be at least 12 inches deep in an IBC setup and another inch of dry media on top.

I have seen many people with great setups asking questions about why their hydroton floats in their growbeds. That's because most hydroton will float, if there is nothing to keep it down, you will have a floating media bed. That's one of the reasons why you need to have one inch of dry media on top.

It is also useful to prevent algae growth and reduce evaporation.

Step 5 – Adding Water

You're now ready to add the water to your tank!

Adding some water or grow media from an already established aquaponics system or pond is the best because it already contains some bacteria.

The next option is plain tap water. Keep in mind that it will take longer for bacteria to populate the system when using tap water.

With tap water, you will have chlorine in it. Turning on your aerator will help to get rid of it, but it can still take several days or even weeks if you have a larger system.

If your water has chloramine, you need to use a reverse osmosis filter or use a carbon filter. Chloramine can't be aired out like chlorine.

If you are using well water, you need to be wary of water hardness and alkalinity. You need to test it and keep it under a certain level. Hardiness of the water will mess with the nutrient availability to the plants. I talk more about hardiness and alkalinity later in the book.

Step 6 – Cycling

To get the desired bacteria, you need to have ammonia in your tank. To create ammonia in your tank, we do something called cycling. There are two types of cycling:

- Cycling with fish (safest).
- Cycling without fish (fastest).

Cycling with Fish

It is possible to cycle by introducing fish and letting them prepare the water. This will take approximately 8-12 weeks, depending on your system.

The fish are the suppliers of the toxic ammonia. If you introduce the fish first, you'll need to monitor the ammonia almost every day. Because there will be no bacteria yet to convert ammonia to nitrites and nitrates. If ammonia rises above the allowable value (see next table), you need to lower the feed you give to the fish or even do a partial water exchange in an emergency.

Most of the time, you will start the system with small fish. Using small fish is never a problem when you are cycling a new system. However, if you use fully grown fish to start the system, you might run into some deadly ammonia, and nitrite spikes before the right number of bacteria are present.

Remember that ammonia levels are at their highest right after feeding.

Some people use goldfish for cycling their system because they are hardy fish. I advise against using goldfish for cycling and just use the fish you intend to grow from the start while they still are fingerlings.

If you are eager to get started as soon as possible, you can cycle without fish in the system.

Cycling Without Fish

This approach requires less monitoring and is faster. The reason for this is simple; you do not have to keep the water levels balanced to keep the fish healthy. You are basically going to manually put ammonia in the system in order to speed up the process.

Because you don't need to worry about the health of the fish now, you can add more ammonia and do this process much more quickly.

Testing is very important! I use the API freshwater test kit. Add some ammonia and allow it to go to 1 or 2ppm.

After a while, you will see an increase in nitrites, and later nitrates will appear. If you see nitrates appear in your system and the ammonium and nitrites are lower than 0.5, you can add your plants and the fish.

You can add your plants in the system sooner, but they wouldn't grow as well because there are no nitrates to feed on.

Important: again, test your system before introducing the fish!

Here are several ways to add ammonia and get the cycling process started:

Urine
Believe it or not, your urine is a good source of ammonia. In fact, urine contains urea, which breaks down to become ammonia. You can add your urine directly to your fish tank if you wish, although it is better to store it for a few days or even a week before you add it. This will allow the urea to break down, and the ammonia can get straight to work.

However, be warned; once you've stored it for several days, it will smell strongly of ammonia.

Urea Fertilizers
You can get urea fertilizer from most agricultural suppliers and nurseries. All you need to do is add it to your tank according to the quantity on the label.

Household Ammonia
You can purchase ammonia from many different stores. Again, you'll need to be careful not to overdose the system. This is the most popular method.

Use Dead Fish
Place a dead fish or two in your tank. As they decompose, they will release ammonia, which the bacteria you are trying to attract will love.

Fish Food
Fish food that is not eaten will break down into ammonia. Therefore, you must be careful not to overfeed your fish when your system is running.

If there is too much ammonia, your bacteria will not be able to keep up with the nitrification, and the levels of ammonia can become dangerous to the fish.

For cycling purposes, it is perfect. Just add some fish food and allow it to break down. You can crush the fish food to have it dissolve faster.

Using the fishless method should ensure that your aquaponics system is ready to start working properly in just a couple of weeks.

Step 7 – Testing

Before you introduce your fish and plants, it is important to test the water.

The levels of ammonia (ppm) change with the pH and temperature of your water. If temperature and pH increases, so does the toxicity of the ammonia. Basically, if you know the pH and the temperature of the water, you will automatically know the level of toxic ammonia.

Temperature	pH				
	6	6.4	6.8	7	7.4
39.2°F (4°C)	200	67	29	18	11
46.4°F (8°C)	100	50	20	13	8
53.6°F (12°C)	100	40	14	9.5	5.9
60.8°F (16°C)	67	29	11	6.9	4.4
68°F (20°C)	50	20	8	5.1	3.2
75.2°F (24°C)	40	15	6.1	3.9	2.4
82.4°F (28°C)	29	12	4.7	2.9	1.8
89.6°F (32°C)	22	8.7	3.5	2.2	1.4

Temperature	pH				
	7.6	7.8	8	8.2	8.4
39.2°F (4°C)	7.1	2.8	1.8	1.1	0.68
46.4°F (8°C)	5.1	2	1.3	0.83	0.5
53.6°F (12°C)	3.7	1.5	0.95	0.61	0.36
60.8°F (16°C)	2.7	1.1	0.71	0.45	0.27
68°F (20°C)	2.1	0.83	0.53	0.34	0.21
75.2°F (24°C)	1.5	0.63	0.4	0.26	0.16
82.4°F (28°C)	1.2	0.48	0.31	0.2	0.12
89.6°F (32°C)	0.89	0.37	0.24	0.16	0.1

Having tilapia in a system at 82°F and your pH is 7.6, then your maximum ammonia level will be 1.2ppm.

When you get a reading from the pH tester, you will see the combined number of ammonia (NH3) and ammonium (NH4). Ammonia is very toxic to fish, while ammonium is not as toxic. This combined number is referred to as Total Ammonia Nitrogen (TAN).

Understanding the difference between the two is crucial to getting to know your total amount of toxic ammonia.

How much ammonia you have depends on the level of your pH and temperature. This is due to the fact that ammonia and ammonium switch between each other under certain circumstances. Ammonia is present with a higher pH when ammonium is present with a lower pH. At a pH of 8, your system contains 50% ammonia and 50% ammonium. If you lower the pH, the less toxic ammonium will stand out.

Example:
Tilapia likes 82°F or 28°C. If you are starting out, you probably have a pH of 8. This means you can only have 0.31ppm of combined ammonia and ammonium in the water. If your system matures and drops to a pH of 6.8, the maximum TAN number shifts to 4.7ppm.

The following tests should also be done on a regular basis once the fish are in the tank:

Ammonia
You can read the maximum levels from the table before.
Normally you would see 0.25-0.5 with low-density systems and 1 to 2ppm with high-density systems.

If you have a high pH level, the toxic ammonia is dominant. Consider lowering your pH levels. The nitrification process will automatically lower the pH level in your system.

Reducing ammonia: lower feed rates and search for dead fish or dead material clogging up your growbed that is reducing the number of nitrifying bacteria.

Ammonium
It is not very toxic to fish and goes combined with ammonia. If your system has a low pH, the less harmful ammonium will be dominant.

pH
Fish prefer 7.5 to 8.5
Plants prefer 6.0 to 6.5
Nitrifying bacteria prefer 7.0 to 8.0

An ideal pH is between 6.5 and 7.5. Don't go lower than 6.5 or higher than 7.5. At the start, your pH will probably be higher than the advised 7.5. Allow some time (few months) for the system to go lower.

pH up: If your system becomes healthy over time, the water will get more acidic, and your pH will drop. When your pH level is too low, bacteria won't be able to convert ammonia into nitrates anymore, and your fish will die. You can use potassium hydroxide and hydrated lime (calcium hydroxide). To increase the pH, you need to use these two together in a 50-50 mixture to not let the one (potassium) overtake the other (calcium).

You can say potassium and calcium fight with each other to overtake one another. Many systems have a potassium deficiency. That's why adding calcium without the additional supplementation of potassium is a bad idea.

pH down: you can use chemical products to bring your pH down, but it's a losing battle. The best thing to do is just wait for the nitrifying bacteria population to grow. If your system is up and running, it will naturally bring your pH down. If you are desperate to bring down your pH, you can use a hydroponic pH down solution or phosphoric acid. Do not drop the pH more than 0.5ppm per day.

Once your bacteria have colonized your grow media or the surface area of your biofilter, your pH will go down naturally.

If the pH rises for some unexpected reason, check your growbeds for solids build-up. Solids will collect in the grow media, and the bacteria will suffocate because they can't get enough oxygen. Bacteria will die, and pH will increase. This is because the nitrifying bacteria automatically lower the pH. With these bacteria gone, the pH will rise.

Nitrite
Ideally, 0ppm. 1ppm is becoming dangerous. This also depends on the kind of fish. Read more about the nitrite spike later in the book.

Nitrate
This feeds your plants and can be as high as 100ppm. Toxicity depends on the fish but is generally very high (160ppm+). You should aim for a minimum of 5ppm and a maximum of 30ppm.

Dissolved Oxygen
You also need to ensure that the fish and plants have enough oxygen. The easiest way to do this is via the aerator you should already have in the fish tank. If fish are constantly coming to the surface gasping for air, it's the sign you don't have enough oxygen in the water. Aim for 5ppm. Some fish, like trout, require more dissolved oxygen.

Your plants need oxygen too. Failing to provide oxygen to the roots will lead to root rot. Healthy roots look white, while roots that are deprived of oxygen are brown. In growbeds, oxygen is supplied by the flood and drain cycle. In DWC, oxygen is supplied through air stones under the floating rafts.

These were the basic tests. In the chapter 'summing up aquaponics,' I will give you more details about nutrients.

Your pH levels will be high during cycling but should settle once bacteria are populating the bio-media or grow media.

Don't add citric acid (lime juice). Some people recommend it to bring down the pH, but it will kill the bacteria in your tank. It will destroy the balance of your aquaponics system!

It is worth noting that concrete will raise the pH level of your water; it is recommended not to let the water come in contact with concrete.

Don't use oyster shells or eggshells to increase the calcium or pH of your system. We already add calcium in the pH up formula; adding calcium without potassium will lead to nutrient imbalances.

Step 8 – Plants

If you added plants while cycling, you would notice they don't grow very fast. This is normal in the beginning because your system is still populating with nitrifying bacteria.

When you add plants, you need to make sure they are as clean as possible. If you want to use plants that were in the soil before, you should visually check each plant to ensure it is disease and bug-free.

Step 9 – Fish

When cycling without fish

When the nitrates start to appear, and the pH level is under 8; (preferably lower), you are ready to add the fish. Of course, the ammonia should be below the advised level (previous table), and the nitrites should be under 0.5ppm.

Adding fish to the tank

First, keep the fish in the bag and place it in the fish tank. The water temperature will slowly equalize between the two. This way, the fish are not shocked when they enter the fish tank.

After a while, open the bag and exchange some water from the fish tank with the water in the bag where the fish are. This will equalize the pH, just as the temperature did. After an hour, you can introduce the fish to your fish tank.

Don't forget that the weight of the fish is calculated on their mature weight even if you add them as fingerlings.

Feeding

Your system is now up and running! You will probably be anxiously looking at it every day. However, even though the plants grow faster, you're not going to be able to see them growing fast just yet.

You will need to make sure they have all the food they need. For this, you need to feed your fish; they will produce the ammonia that the bacteria can turn into nitrates and other nutrients for the plants.

We have already talked and calculated the amount of feed we need to give to our fish in relation to the available growing area. But because smaller ones eat less, I have made some calculations to account for that.

To give you an idea of how much food is required, an adult tilapia fish will eat approximately 1.5-2% of its body weight per day. When they are fingerlings, they require 6-10% of their body weight.

Fish size (g)	Feed type	Feed size	Feeding rate	Feeding frequency
		(mm)	(% body weight)	(no./day)
0–1	Powder/crumble	0.2–1	30–10	8 to satiation
1–5	Crumble	1–1.5	10–6	5–6
5–20	Extruded, floating	1.5–2	6–4	4
20–100	Extruded, floating	2	4–3	3
100–250	Extruded, floating	3	3–2	2
>250	Extruded, floating	4	2–1.5	2

Tilapia feeding rates

Life stage	Weight (g)
First feeding larvae	
Fry	0.02–1.0
Fingerlings	1.0–10.0
Juveniles	10.0–25.0
Adults	25–200
	>200
Broodstock	

Tilapia weight and life stage

This is different for every species of fish.

This means if you have 25 adult tilapia with a total of 25 pounds (11.3kg), you'll need approximately .375 pounds of fish food a day (170 grams).
Having 25 tilapia fingerlings would mean they weigh a total of 5.3 ounces (0.2 ounces per fingerling). You would need to feed them 0.32 ounces (6% of their body weight).

If, for any reason, your fish isn't eating, they are probably stressed. This is because the water is not balanced properly, the temperature is wrong, or they are struggling for oxygen. There is only one solution:

Test, test, and test!

In the beginning, you should run these tests at least weekly:

- pH levels.
- Ammonia.
- Nitrite.
- Water temperature.
- Visible pests.

Fish

Getting your system ready is exciting, but the best part of any aquaponics system is when you select the appropriate fish.

There's a good chance you already know the answer to this question.

Virtually any fish can be successfully introduced to an aquaponics system. The most important thing is to ensure that the fish and the plants have similar needs in terms of temperature and pH levels; this will make it much easier to keep both healthy.

It is worth noting that freshwater fish and leafy crops such as lettuce or herbs are generally considered to be the most productive. But systems that have a lot of fish can be very good at providing the nutrients needed to nurture nutrient hungry plants such as peppers and tomatoes.

It's important to choose a fish that's thriving in your local climate. It doesn't make sense to keep trout in Florida or tilapia in Canada. Always choose a fish that's used to your local climate, if you don't want to spend money on additional heating or cooling.

Here are some of the most common and potentially best choices:

Tilapia

Tilapia has become a common choice for aquaculture and aquaponic systems. This means the price has been decreasing, which helps to make them affordable and the right choice for your system. They might not be attractive for commercial reasons because of the low local price.

Perhaps more important is the fact that these fish are very hardy and tolerant of changes in your system. They are known to be very hardy and can survive in low oxygen water (3ppm).

The Nile tilapia

They are great if you're struggling to get your pH level or temperature right. It's also good to know they are fast-growing, helping to ensure your plants get all the nutrition they need.

In some place's tilapia is banned (California); they are getting into the local ecosystem and pushing out native species. Check with your local government to learn if they are allowed.

Tilapia will usually take 240 days (8 months) to reach one pound. Tilapia like water that is in the range of 75° to 90°F (24-32°C). If it goes lower, they'll become dormant, and below 55°F (13°C) equals death. If you live in a cold climate, it might not be a good choice to choose tilapia.

Bluegill

These are also a good choice if you're struggling to monitor the temperature of your water effectively. They are also very tolerant of other fish, allowing you to keep more than one species of fish in your system if you wish.

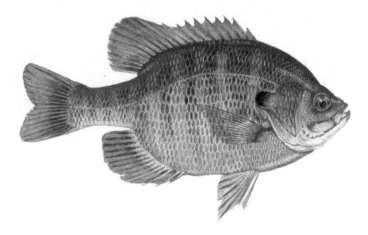

The bluegill

Bluegills can grow as long as 10 inches (25cm) in the space of 6 months. In fact, this fish can live to be 10 or 11 years old.
They do need coverage to feel comfortable in their tank and prefer pH levels of 7. However, they are not strictly a tropical fish so they can survive in a range of temperatures. Ideally, you should have the water at 65°F (18°C), but they can handle it as low as 50°F (10°C) or as high as 80°F (27°C).

Crappie

These fish taste excellent and are always in demand by restaurants. They are also easy to control and maintain in an aquaponics system. This allows you to get large fish that can be sold to the local restaurants while your plants benefit from their waste.

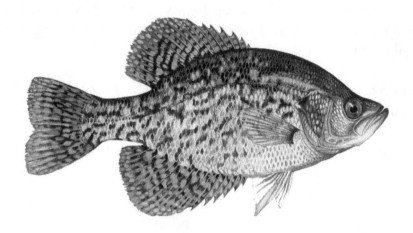

A crappie

The crappie likes the pH between 7 and 7.5, with a water temperature of 70° to 75°F (21-24°C). They usually grow fast, reaching 1lb within the first year.

Koi

These are not normally eaten, but they do have a very long life span and are very resistant to parasites. This makes them difficult to kill even if you're struggling to get the parameters right in your system.

Koi prefer water temperatures of 35° to 85°F (2-30°C); that makes them very easy to keep happy. These are also great at eating algae, which may be important if you're suffering from an algae problem.

Koi do take between 3 and 4 years to reach as long as 24 inches (60cm). These fish are more for aesthetics than to feed yourself with. If you do have a koi pond, you can hook it up to your system.

Koi fish

Trout

Trout is undoubtedly one of the most widely farmed fish in the world, majorly because it is a delicious fish.

The best one of these to use in your aquaponics system is the rainbow trout. This isn't because they are the prettiest ones. The simple fact is that rainbow trout are the hardiest type of trout. This makes them easier to grow for aquaculture.

Are you living in a cool climate? Don't you worry, they prefer water temperatures between 48 and 59°F (9 and 15°C). Temperatures over 77°F (25°C) is lethal for the rainbow trout.

Rainbow trout are used to living in flowing rivers or small streams. They like water movement, so try to oversize your pump to replicate this environment for optimal growth. They do need more dissolved oxygen than other fish (aim for 8ppm).

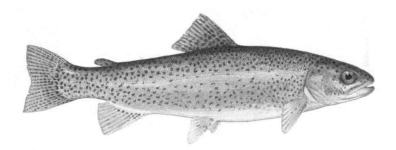

Rainbow trout

If you plan on using rainbow trout, I recommend reading this research paper of small-scale trout farming:
https://www.howtoaquaponic.com/trout-farming

Catfish

Catfish are great for the aquaponics system, although, after adapting to the tanks, they will grow fairly quickly.

These fish are so adaptable that they know how to survive in a very harsh environment like polluted ponds.

You'll also appreciate the fact that catfish are comfortable with water temperatures of between 75-86°F (23-30°C).

These are not the fastest-growing fish; they can be 1 pound in 18 months.

Catfish like to swim at the bottom of the tank. Therefore, keep your stocking densities low.

Channel Catfish

Goldfish

The (golden) standard for beginners. This is not a fish you generally use for eating. But they are the most popular aquarium fish and are exceptionally cheap. They eat crustaceans, insects, and a selection of plants. The more you feed them, the more waste they produce, which will benefit your plants.

They prefer water of 74°F (23°C), making it difficult to keep them warm in winter.

A goldfish

Pacu

These are more likely to react badly to changes in your system, although they are tolerant of higher pH levels.

They need a varied diet but can be stocked in high enough quantities. The Pacu is probably not the best choice for anyone who is new to aquaponics.

Pacu generally live in 80 to 85°F (26 to 29°C) water although they can tolerate an additional 5°F (3°C) in each direction. They should reach plate size in roughly 9 months.

Pacu fish

Angelfish or guppies

Guppies and other ornamental fish are generally very pretty to look at. They are also very good at adapting their diet to what is available. This makes them a good choice if you're struggling with the time to care for and feed your fish on a regular basis.

They are considered difficult to kill and are one of the cheapest fish you can buy, making them a great option for an indoor aquaponics system (because they are small and pretty). They are used in small scale living room aquaponic setups.

Of course, they are not for eating. They prefer temperatures between 75 and 85°F (24-30°C).

Guppies

Fish troubleshooting

We all know it's important to keep your fish happy. But what means a happy fish? A happy fish likes no stress, gentle changes in pH and temperature. If any of these changes abruptly in any way, the fish becomes stressed.

Avoiding stress is very important to keep the slime layer of a fish intact. If a fish lives under constant stress, the slime layer will become thin and make it more susceptible to parasites and harmful bacteria.

Testing water quality often is a great way of reducing stress for the fish. The topic of water quality brings us to the next common causes of fish deaths in aquaponics.

Nitrite poisoning

Nitrite poisoning usually happens at the beginning of the cycling process. The bacteria that convert ammonia to nitrite are the first to develop. The other bacteria that convert nitrite to nitrates will develop at a later stage. The time between these two stages is dangerous for your fish. The nitrite levels will be high because they can't be converted to nitrate yet. Nitrite is very toxic to fish, which will result in their death at around 0.5ppm, depending on the fish.

Symptoms are fish gasping for air, loss of appetite, and heavy breathing through the gills. It is similar to oxygen deprivation but in this case, there is plenty of oxygen in the water. It is also called brown blood disease because the blood isn't able to carry oxygen, so it turns brown instead of red.

Oxygen deprivation

Oxygen deprivation is another problem that is frequently occurring. In this case, there is not enough oxygen in the water to supply the fish. The oxygen dissolved in the water is depleted. Dissolved oxygen will lower when the water temperature rises, so look out for your DO level when summer comes around.

Tilapia are used to living in warm water and have adapted themselves to living in oxygen-deprived water (3ppm). Trout, on the other hand, needs lots of oxygen to survive (8+ppm).

Symptoms are fish gasping for air at the surface, very slow movement, and reduced appetite.

Fish appetite

Fish appetite changes when temperature increases or decreases. For example, koi fish will stop eating in winter and burn their fat until they resume eating in spring.

When the temperature decreases, the metabolism of the fish slows down. They are not able to eat as much. Less feed means less nutrients for the plants, which will impact plant growth.

If you want a year-round production, you need to keep the temperature constant, so fish always have an appetite and eat their food.

Best plants

We can divide plants into two categories:

- Vegetative plants.
- Fruiting plants.

Vegetating plants are plants like lettuce, kale, spinach, and basil. Vegetative plants don't require many nutrients to grow. They can thrive with low nutrient levels. That's because vegetative plants require mostly nitrogen to grow.

Fruiting plants, on the other hand, need rich nutrient water to produce their fruits. Fruiting plants need nitrogen, phosphorus, and potassium to grow big fruit.

If you are familiar with hydroponics, you will know about the most important nutrients called N-P-K.

- N stand for nitrogen.
- P stands for phosphorous.
- K stands for potassium.

Nitrogen is needed for leaf growth, while more phosphorous and potassium are needed for fruit production. Because you will have plenty of nitrogen in the beginning (nitrates), it's easier to start growing leafy vegetables and move to fruiting crops later.

The nutrient potassium is supplemented into your system once the pH starts to drop (in combination with calcium). So, growing fruiting crops makes more sense when you have an established system where you already have supplemented potassium.

Your nitrate levels should go up and down all the time. If you have a healthy system and want to increase the available nutrients, you should increase fish feed.

After you feed the fish, you should see a spike in ammonia, then nitrites, and then nitrates. The conversion from ammonia to nitrates can happen in a few hours. The faster this is completed while still maintaining optimal feeding rate (60-100grams/m²/day) in DWC, the healthier your system is.

Leafy Lettuce

This is one of the easiest plants to grow in a raft style system. The reason for this is the ease of access to nutrients, and they don't need support.

Lettuce

They are also tolerant of pH changes (between 6 and 7). Having their roots in oxygenated nutrient-rich liquid all the time is the perfect environment. It likes a temperature between 45 – 70°F (7-21°C).

Kale

Kale is very similar to leafy lettuce and can offer the same advantages to the dedicated grower. This is also a good grower because of access to water.

The fact that it tastes good and is full of vitamins is a bonus. Expect to harvest your first plants after 6 – 8 weeks. It likes temperature between 40 – 65°F (5 – 18°C)

Swiss Chard

Swiss chard is resistant to parasites and other diseases. With a little vigilance, you should have a grown crop in just a few weeks. You'll need to keep the temperature around 70°F to 85°F (25 – 30°C).

Swiss Chard

Basil

Basil flourishes in soil filled with water. Therefore, it will do well in a grow bed and in floating rafts. It can cope with drops in temperature, although it may slightly affect its growth rate. It likes 65 – 80°F (18 – 26°C)

It can be cut to harvest, and it will regrow again. It's best to cut a maximum of 3 times before using another basil plant. It's best to cut 6 inches from the base of the plant and leave some leaves for its regeneration.

Watercress

This plant naturally grows in wet areas, so an aquaponics media bed or raft system will make it feel very comfortable. It is also a very fast grower; you'll be surprised at how quickly watercress grows.

Unless you keep it small, you'll be looking to give away or sell your crop. It'll be too much to eat yourself.

You should be able to start harvesting in just 3 – 4 weeks. It likes 60°F (15°C)

Watercress in a growbed

Bok Choi

This is a member of the cabbage family with a wide variety of names. As a cabbage, it will need a higher level of nutrients, and you'll need to maximize your fish stocking.

It is worth growing as it can be ready to eat in just 6 – 8 weeks. It likes temperatures ranging from 50 – 70°F (10 – 21°C).

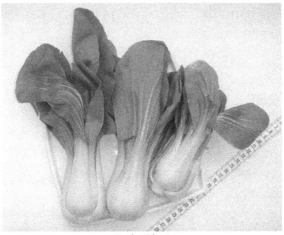

Bok Choi

Others

- Tomatoes.
- Peppers.
- Cauliflower.
- Broccoli.
- Beans.
- Peas.
- Cabbage.
- Cucumbers.
- Squash.

Most of these plants in this list have are top-heavy and, therefore, require a strong root system. That's why it's best to grow these in a grow bed or dutch buckets where the roots and the media allows the plant to stay upright with the help of trellises.

You could grow these in floating rafts, but then you need to build sufficient support for them.

It's not unusual to see plants with big roots in a floating raft setup, but it's just less common.

Pests

The lack of soil in your aquaponics setup means that there is a reduced risk of parasites eating the roots of your plants. Unfortunately, this doesn't mean that no pests can attack your plants. The only way this would be possible is if you were to have a sealed room and carefully control every entry and exit point to ensure no pest could get into the space.

This will not be a viable option if your aquaponics system is outside. Even inside, this is difficult to achieve on a standard budget.

Possible Pests

Here is a list of possible pests. Afterward, I will give some tips on how to get rid of them organically.

Aphids

These tiny black or sometimes green dots can quickly suck the nutrients out of any plant. They walk along the stems and literally suck the sap from the plant. This removes the nutrients and will make your plant ill. Eventually, it will die.

Some of the most commonly mentioned aphids are greenfly and blackfly. They can breed incredibly quickly. It is important to treat them as soon as you find them; you don't want these pests spreading over to the rest of your crops.

An aphid (can be green or black)

Caterpillars

You already know what a caterpillar is. On its way to becoming a beautiful butterfly, it will chomp through every green leaf it can find.

A lettuce eating caterpillar

On the plus side, these pests are relatively easy to pick off and remove; simply check the underside of your leaves where they usually hide.

Squash Bugs

Unsurprisingly these bugs are most commonly found on squash plants; they may not be an issue to you if you're not growing any kind of squash.

They look very similar to the stink bug, are approximately ½ inch long, and have flat backs. The squash bug is gray and brown with orange stripes on the bottom of their abdomen.

A squash bug (picture courtesy of Donna Brunet)

You'll usually find them on the underside of your leaves in a group. They can fly but generally prefer to walk on your plants. These bugs will destroy the flow of nutrients to your plants.

Mealybugs

This is yet another pest that multiplies rapidly once they find a home. They tend to prefer warmer environments. Your aquaponics setup will probably be ideal for growth! The amount of damage they do will depend on the number of pests you have; early detection is crucial. Mealybugs are oval insects approximately ¼inch long and covered with a white or gray wax.

A mealybug

Cutworms

The cutworm is the larvae of several different species of adult moths. They will generally hibernate for the winter months; unless your aquaponics system is warm enough to discourage this.

A black cutworm

Once they finish hibernating, they will emerge and start eating the leaves of your plants. They generally feed at dusk; this is the best time to see them in action. They are effectively caterpillars but are often considered grubs. The exact size and look will depend on the species.

Hornworms

You're most at risk of getting them if you have tomatoes. They are green, generally fat, and look like caterpillars.

The adult moth lays eggs on the underside of your leaves in the late spring. These will hatch in less than a week. You'll then have larvae, which will start to eat your plants for the next 4 – 6 weeks until nothing is left but the stems.

A hornworm

They will generally go into a cocoon for the winter, but if your aquaponics system is warm enough, they may only do this for a couple of weeks. They can then transform into moths and lay more eggs to feed on your plants.

What might surprise you is the size of the hornworm; it can be as much as 5 inches long! They are pale green and have white and black markings. They also have a horn at their rear. Although this looks dangerous, they are not capable of stinging you.

You'll find dark green droppings on the top of your leaves; this will tell you the hornworm is present; turn your leaf over to see them.

Dealing with Pests

Recognizing the pest is only the first step; you also need to be able to get rid of the problem without damaging your system. It should go without saying that regular pesticides and other chemicals cannot be used. They may kill the pests, but they are also extremely likely to make your fish ill or perhaps even kill them. That's why you need to know the best natural methods for dealing with pests.

Having a greenhouse where soil-based plants are located is a bad idea. Pests could use the soil as a breeding ground before they move on to your aquaponics setup.

Growing your own produce from seeds will drastically eliminate the possible pests that are on a plant. The plants you buy from your local dealer could be filled with pests already.

Sap Suckers

One of the best natural remedies for sap suckers is to spray your plants with chili or garlic spray. However, these can affect the taste of your crop and in large quantities, can make it uncomfortable for the plants or the fish.

Moderation is the key. Alternatively, you can use beneficial insects, which are discussed later in this chapter.

Caterpillars

The simplest way of getting rid of caterpillars is to spray a substance called Bacillus thuringiensis. You should be able to get this in your local garden store.

It is a natural soil-borne bacteria that kills caterpillars and their larvae. Fortunately, it is completely safe for your aquaponics system and your plants.

Mold & Fungus

Potassium bicarbonate is excellent at destroying virtually all molds and fungus. You can spray a little directly onto any affected plants and the ones immediately next to them.

Snails

Snails are not good for the system. They are in the water and can eat the roots of your plants. They also feed on the nitrifying bacteria, which will lead to less efficient nitrification. Use red ear sunfish to control the snails. Preferably under the rafts in DWC (they won't eat your roots).

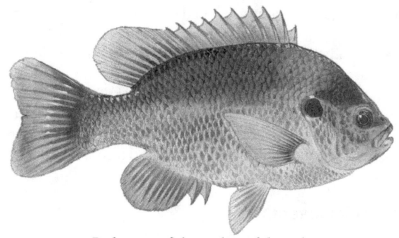

Red ear sunfish eats harmful snails

Slugs

You shouldn't have a problem with slugs as they should find it difficult to get into your aquaponics system. However, difficult is not the same as impossible.

Slug damage

If slugs do get into your grow beds, you can do three things:

- Flood the entire growbed to the top so the slugs will drown.
- Add a small saucer filled with beer. The slugs will be attracted by the smell and will climb into the saucer. They won't make it out of the saucer and will drown.
- Handpick them off your plants and feed them to the fish.

Beneficial Insects

Another great way of dealing with pests in your aquaponics system is to use beneficial insects. As the name suggests, these are insects that will help your system by eating the pests that do damage. It's a good idea to have them in your system year-round. That means when there will be an outbreak, they might be able to limit it or negate the outbreak.

Although it might not be easy to introduce them to your outdoor system, it's preferably done indoors or in a greenhouse where they are contained.

You can order live animals online on sites like Amazon, insectsales.com, or a local organic gardening store.

Some of the best ones to consider are:

Ladybugs

These are great at getting rid of aphids before they can do any real damage. One ladybug can consume as many as 5,000 aphids per year!

A ladybug

Parasitic Wasp

This tiny wasp doesn't sting. It will lay its eggs in the body of an aphid. The baby wasp eats the inside of the aphid before emerging to repeat the process.

The Parasitic Wasp

Praying Mantis

These slightly strange looking creatures are excellent at eating aphids, caterpillars, potato beetles, leafhoppers, hornworms, squash bugs, and pretty much any pest that could be a problem for your aquaponics setup.

A praying mantis

Lacewings

These are good at attacking virtually all types of aquaponic pests. You'll find they are very good at eating aphids, mealybugs, whitefly, and even thrips. They can eat as many as 100 aphids per week. They also work best at night when most of the pests are active.

A lacewing

It's worth noting that if you had a 1,000 square foot greenhouse, you'd need approximately 2,000 lacewings. You can get these from most biological insect vendors, or you can try planting flowers that attract lacewings near your aquaponics system.

Good flowers to plant are fennel, dill, coriander, dandelion, and angelica. They also like brightly-lit windows.

Spider Mite Predators

The tiny spider mite can suck the nutrients out of 200 different plants. Fortunately, you can solve the issue by introducing the bright orange spider mite predator. They may only live for roughly 45 days, but they can consume as many as 20 spider mites each day!

Aphid Predator Midge

These tiny little bugs look like small mosquitoes. They can sniff out aphid colonies, and then they lay their eggs next to them. Within a few days, the larva will hatch and eat the aphids. The aphid predator midge can consume as many as 15 aphids a day.

A Midge

Nematodes

These are natural parasites that are so small you can only see them with a microscope. They can kill approximately 250 different types of larvae. You can mix these with your water, and they will kill any pests that spend time in the grow bed.

Tips for Getting Started

There is a lot of information to take in before you can get your aquaponics system successfully up and running. Therefore, it is important to follow the steps described earlier and use patience. Once you've established a system, you'll be able to modify your approach, materials, and technique to grow virtually any plant and breed any fish.

Here are some great tips to make your aquaponics system is a success.

Temperature
When you're first starting out, it can be difficult to maintain the temperature at the same time as you manage all the other elements of your setup. Therefore, it is advisable to choose fish that are comfortable in the average temperature where you live.

It is much easier to heat up water than to cool it down. It may be preferable to buy fish that prefer warm water and purchase a water heater to help maintain the temperature instead of pouring ice in your fish tank.

If you live in a cold area and want to have warm water fish with a floating raft system, you should insulate the bottom of your floating raft with insulation panels.

In the following illustration, you will see a floating raft setup with added insulation. Insulation can be added all around the troughs but is the most effective at the bottom.

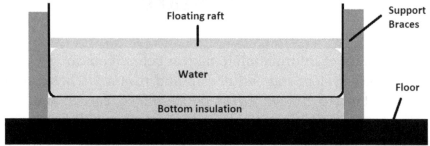

Insulating a floating raft system

Separate the Fish

Baby fish (fingerlings) must be kept separate from adult fish. If you don't, they are likely to be eaten by them.

This is important if you are breeding or restocking fish. However, you should separate the fish into another tank but still have it connected to the aquaponics system. Every bit of fish waste can help your plants flourish.

Warm-blooded animals in aquaponics

Never use any warm-blooded animal like ducks in your aquaponic system. Not even their manure. They will introduce the bacteria called E. Coli into your system, which can make you sick. The fish are coldblooded, so they are not a problem.

The Overflow

Build an overflow from your growbed to the fish tank. This will provide you with a warning that something is wrong. You can even connect it to a sensor to ensure you are aware of the problem.

Clean your growbeds

If you measure high pH and ammonia levels even after you stopped feeding the fish for a while, you need to check your growbeds.

Rotten organic material will create zones that are deprived of oxygen. This means that the bacteria will die in that part of the growbed. Which will harm the nitrification process. Resulting in lower available BSA, higher pH, and elevated ammonia levels.

Having one or more dead fish in your system increases the level of ammonia.

Electrical Protection
Your aquaponics setup relies on electricity to run the pump, lights, and sometimes to keep the water warm. You need to consider the likelihood of a power failure and what back-up system you can have in place, such as battery-operated pumps or even solar power to top up the batteries.

If you have a bigger system, it's not a bad idea to have a small bilge pump that pumps the water around the system once the power goes out. To make this, you will need:

- 12V Battery.
- Charge controller.
- Battery charger or solar panel.
- 12V bilge pump.
- Detection device for when the power is out.

Plug the power loss detector in the plug and wire up the bilge pump to the 12V battery. Once the power loss detector senses that the power is out, the bilge pump will start to pump. Murray Hallam has an excellent video about this on his YouTube channel called: "aphids, murray cod and backups."

You should, of course, ensure that all your electrical equipment is as far away from the water as possible; unless it is approved to go in the water. An electric shock is just as dangerous to your fish as it is to you.

Start small

It is essential to start your system small. This will allow you to make mistakes and learn from them without costing you a fortune and losing your fish. You can even set up more than one system at the start and combine them later.

Once you've established a successful small system, you can move on to a larger setup.

Chemicals

Don't forget that the chemicals you usually use on plants may not be safe in an aquaponics system. Anything you add to the system will affect both the plants and the fish. You can only use natural products.

If the pests get really bad, you can resort to OMRI (Organic Materials Review Institute) certified products. Which, in moderation, won't harm your fish.

Don't lose curious fish

I hear it happening all the time, people losing their fish through the inlet of the pump. There is a simple solution to this. Use a net to cover the pump or use a net pot and attach it to the pump's inlet. That way, curious fish can't go in the inlet and become instant sushi.

Make sure the pump inlet is free of any debris. If not, it will have reduced suction, which will lead to damage inside the pump.

Adding redworms

Redworms are very cheap to buy or cultivate yourself. They have been shown to be effective at reducing waste build-up in grow beds. They won't drown in your grow beds as long as you use flood and drain.

They will eat the solids that are inside your beds. They excrete usable nutrients for the plant to use (mineralization). If you have enough redworms, you may only need to clean your grow bed once every five years.

A few redworms

Root rot

If your roots start to rot, then you're going to have plants die. Therefore, it is essential to pick it up as soon as possible and resolve the issue. Root rot occurs when your roots don't get enough oxygen or when you have bad solids filtration.

You need to make sure there is plenty of oxygen in your system (min 5ppm).

You can check for root rot by looking at the roots of your plants. If it is slimy and has a brown color, then you know that your roots aren't doing well. Ideally, the roots of the plant need to be white.

Obvious case of root rot

Common Problems to Avoid

Establishing an aquaponics system takes time, patience, knowledge, and most importantly, trial and error.

Being aware of the most common mistakes will make it easier for you to avoid making these and build a successful system.

Access to The Fish

You'll notice some fish tanks are designed with the grow beds on top of the fish tanks. This can save on pipework but will not help you access your fish. The same can be said if you build the fish tank in a location that is difficult to access.

If you can't get into the fish tank, you can't check when a fish is ill, and there will be no space to do some plumbing. This can cause a serious issue if you need to act quickly and can't get into your tank. You must consider access before you start setting up your system.

Iron deficiency

This is one element that is often overlooked but is essential to the health of your plants and their ability to do photosynthesis. Iron is needed in a plant to produce chlorophyll, which results in green leaves. If there is an iron deficiency, the leaves will start to become yellow. The deficiency is called chlorosis.

It is advisable to purchase an iron test to check the iron levels at least once a month.

If iron levels are low (1.5 to 2ppm), you can add some with a chelated iron supplement (to 3ppm) that can be bought online or in a hydroponics store. You can spot iron deficiency if the leaves are turning yellow instead of green while the veins are still green. It will show up on the new leaves (top of the plant).

Iron will become less available to the plant if the pH is higher than 6.5. That's another reason why you need to keep your pH between 6.5 and 7.5.

A leaf turning yellow on new leaves could be a sign of iron deficiency

Potassium deficiency

Potassium is needed by the plant to regulate its water uptake. Potassium is provided by the fish food but is barely enough to run the system because fish need potassium too. A deficiency in potassium will lead to reduced resistance to pests, unhealthy roots, and smaller fruits.

The symptoms of potassium deficiency are scorching and burning leaf tips and yellowing of the leaf between the veins. This deficiency is most common in fruiting plants. Symptoms will show on the lower leaves first because they were the first to grow (oldest growth first).

That's why I recommend only planting fruiting plants when your system is of age or has mineralization installed.

Potassium deficient tomato plant (yellowing at the leaf tip)

Do not confuse potassium deficiency with nitrate or iron deficiency. You can test nitrate deficiency with a simple test kit, and you can rule out iron deficiency to look at the place the yellowing leaves occur. If the yellowing occurs in the lower leaves, it's potassium deficiency. If it occurs in new leaf growth, it's iron deficiency.

When your pH is low, you will be supplementing with a 50/50 mix of potassium hydroxide and hydrated lime. Like previously said, the hydrated lime (calcium) will raise the pH, but the potassium hydroxide will avoid that calcium takes the upper hand.

When you don't need to lower your pH but have a potassium deficiency, you need to supplement potassium that is pH neutral. One of these supplements is kelp or kelp meal. You can spray it on the leaves or supplement it in the water.

If you have a large deficiency, consider using potassium sulfate dissolved in the water of the system. It's much stronger than kelp or kelp meal. The amount depends on the volume of the system and the strength of the solution.

pH Issue

If your pH levels are off (6.5 to 7.5 is good), it is important to adjust them to ensure your fish and plants are comfortable. However, this is something that must be done gradually. You should not drop or raise the pH by more than .5 per day. If you do, you're likely to put the fish under stress; that's not a good plan as stress will reduce their slime layer, which is protecting them from diseases.

Algae

It is worth talking a little more about algae. In the long run, the level of algae should stabilize, but when you're first getting started, it can be a real pain.

Green algae are the most common issue in aquaponics. Too much of it is likely to make your water appear green and can even block your pipes and filters in extreme cases.

But this is only part of the problem! Algae can also accumulate in your grow beds and steal the oxygen that is vital to your system.

It can also affect the pH of your system. It can cause the pH to swing in both directions. It can make remedial action difficult, especially if you're new to aquaponics. It is best to watch the pH for a day or two before reacting. If it's low in the morning but high late in the afternoon, you probably have an algae problem.

To control the algae, you'll need to add shade to your fish tank and exposed water. The lack of sunlight will stop the algae from reproducing.

It's important if you are planning to use grow beds, that the top layer that's exposed to the sun will not get wet. This is to discourage algae from growing in your grow beds. Place 1 inch of dry expanded clay or river rock on the top of your grow beds to block out sunlight.

It is also possible to add organic humic acid. It's an organic darkening agent. It will darken the water, preventing the algae from getting the light they need to grow.

If you are running a DWC system, you can add shrimps under your floating rafts. They eat the algae and other organic matter that will be in your troughs. You should supply them with some objects to hide from each other because they are territorial. You can use the leftovers of your building materials like piping scraps.

High nitrates will also lead to algae growth. If your nitrates are over 30ppm, I recommend installing denitrification. I will talk more about denitrification in the 'advanced' chapter.

Leaving the system to do its work

Once you've got the system working and the fish are doing well while the plants are growing, you need to continue to monitor them. One of the most surprising and common issues is when people leave their systems completely alone if everything is running properly once the fish and the plants are happy. In theory, this is correct, but it is unlikely to be the case in practice.

An aquaponics system is generally less work than the traditional approach to gardening and crop growing. But you still need to monitor the system and make the appropriate changes. Forget this, and your system will have a problem; faster than you think.

Adding Water

The quality of the water going into your system must be excellent. Choose rainwater or water from an already successful aquaponics system when you are starting out.

Failing this, you need tap water. The pH should be between 6.5 and 7.5, and the temperature between 64 and 86 degrees (18° and 30°C). Depending on the tolerance of the fish, you have chosen to add to your tank.

If you are topping up your system with tap water, only top up a small amount. The chlorine or chloramine will kill some bacteria. If you put in a small percentage, you will be fine.

I can't stress this enough; always test your water for pH, and nitrites before putting fish in it. I've heard stories from people who didn't test their water before they put their fish in, and the results weren't good.

Grow Media

We've already mentioned the different types of growing media. Many people are tempted to purchase a local option because it is cheaper (and that's a good thing).

Whatever option you choose, it is essential to use one that is pH neutral and doesn't have limestone in it. This will ensure you have the perfect conditions for bacteria to multiply and your plants to grow.

Earthquakes

Luckily, this might not be applicable to you. If you live in an active area for earthquakes, you need to know there might be a tear forming in your piping or fish tank. In case of an earthquake, how little it can be, check for tears and leaks in your system.

Solid foundations

Having a solid foundation for your system is a must. I have seen so many great setups without a proper foundation. Once it rains or there is a leak in one of the pipes, the sand under the fish tank or growbeds erodes away, which will result in disaster.

Don't be that person, place a solid foundation. Digging down and using cinder blocks or gravel to allow good drainage will put you in a good position.

Sumps

Sumps are used to create the lowest point in your system. From there, the water is pumped back to the fish tank. Because sumps are the lowest point in your system, they are partially or fully underground. If you live in an area where there is a lot of rainfall, the water table can rise and push the sump tank up or even crack it. This will lead to disaster.

Having your sump topped up to at least half (I recommend ¾), would alleviate this problem. The water in the IBC will have the same force of the groundwater surrounding it, so it doesn't get pushed up or cracks.

Another recommendation about sumps is that it's better to have the sump filled up as high as possible without causing any spills. Having a high-water level will result in less head height for your pump to deliver. Less head height means more flow and less energy usage.

Rootbound

Most of the time, rootbound appears in growbeds. Rootbound means there are too many roots in the growbed. The roots will block the siphon from doing its job. The roots will also decrease draining speed, which results in longer cycle times. Furthermore, solids will become trapped in the root mass, which will result in more anaerobic zones.

If roots become a problem in your growbeds, it's best to remove them before your nitrifying bacteria die. Once your pH is starting to rise, you should check for problems in your growbed(s).

Cleaning out growbeds

Cleaning out growbeds is not a fun activity. That's why you would like to do them all in one go. But that might not be a good idea.

It's better to clean out one growbed at a time and wait a few weeks before cleaning out the next one. If you clean out the growbeds all at once, your bacteria population might suffer. If you do them one by one, your bacteria population will keep the nutrient supply stable.

Nitrite spike

The nitrite spike, also known as nitrite poisoning, is a problem that occurs when starting your system with adult fish before there are bacteria present.

Your system needs to populate two different kinds of bacteria to convert ammonia to nitrates. The first ones are called Nitrosomonas and convert the ammonia to nitrites. They colonize the system first and reproduce faster than the other bacteria. The other bacteria are called Nitrobacter, which converts the toxic nitrite to beneficial nitrate. These bacteria are slower in colonizing the system and slower to reproduce.

If you stock the fish without having the second bacteria (Nitrobacter) to convert nitrites to nitrates, you will have a spike in nitrites. This is very toxic to the fish and will lead to dying fish.

Not cleaning out your growbeds or cleaning out all your growbeds at one time can also result in nitrite poisoning.

Fish gasping for air or faster gill movement than usual, while the dissolved oxygen in the water is high, is an indication of nitrite poisoning.

MildewCide

If you decide to paint your system, make sure you are not using a paint that has the chemical mildewcide in it. It is used as mildew prevention on newly painted surfaces.

Once it comes in contact with your water, it will leech into the water and will make your fish and plans sick or even kill them.

Advanced Techniques

Once you understand the basics of aquaponics and manage to get your system working, it's time to take it a step further. This can involve upgrading to a bigger setup, or you may wish to change the fish and plants you are using. You may choose to operate two separate systems, as this will allow you to experiment with different fish and plants without risking your original setup.

The following advanced tips can also help you to improve the current setup you already have.

Grow More Without Extra Space

If you don't have a lot of space, but you want to improve your yield, then you need to look at building a vertical aquaponics system. The only limit to how high you can go is the height of the room you have available and can reach up to.

The water must be pumped through all the trays, and the usual rules regarding the number of fish / volumes of water and grow bed space still apply. You can use an NFT or DFT system for this. A lettuce needs approximately 0.7ft of space to grow.

If you follow bright agrotech on YouTube, you will see him using grow towers with bio media in them called Zip grow towers. It's basically a variant of the Matala filter media. He uses the media in the grow towers to house the bacteria (like a drip biofilter).

Artificial Lights

When growing commercially, you need to calculate how much power you are going to use. You can't hide the fact that the sun is a huge source of energy for your plants.

If you grow indoors, you need to be prepared for a big electrical bill because of the grow lights you will need. This isn't such a big issue with greenhouses or hobby farmers although greenhouses can use artificial lights as supplementation.

How to calculate energy costs?
I have a double T5 fluorescent grow light that consumes 100 watts of power and a pump that runs on 50 watts. The T5 grow light is on for 12 hours a day, and the pump is running 24/7.

First, I calculate how many watts a day I require to run this.

Light: 100 *watts x* 12 *hours* = 1200 *watt hours per day*
Pump: 50 *watts x* 24 *hours* = 12000 *watt hours per day*

1200*wh* + 1200*wh* = 2400*wh consumed in one day*

Then I calculate how much that is in Kwh.

$$\frac{2400wh}{1000} = 2.4kwh \ consumed \ in \ one \ day$$

Next, you need to figure out how much you pay for one Kwh in your area. Let's say it's $0.12 for one Kwh, which is the national average in the U.S.

How much does it cost per day?

$0.12 *x* 2.4*kwh* = $0.288

How much does it cost per month?

$$\$0.288 \; x \; 30 = \$8.64 \; each \; month$$

This will be half if we don't use the T5 light. Imagine the savings on a commercial system if we use the energy of the sun.

Go Solar

You need to figure the amount of total energy your system requires before you can comfortably start using solar power.

Getting solar panels is not enough. You'll need to have at least one battery for running at night, a charge controller, and in most cases, an inverter that transforms the 12/24 volts DC to usable 110 volts AC; to run your pumps and possibly grow lights.

If you get DC pumps and DC LED lights, you don't need an inverter. You can then run your pumps and lights directly from the battery, which is more efficient.

This is not something you want to do as a beginner to aquaponics. Setting up solar panels requires an investment in all the necessary gear you need to power your system. The average panel will generate between 200 and 300 watts of power.

This then must be channeled into batteries while being used by your system, and you need to be sure that it stores enough energy to run the system when the sun goes down. It will be essential to do your calculation and have mains back up before you start relying on just solar power.

Discussing the entirety of an off-grid system would be a whole book on its own and goes beyond the scope of this book. There are great tutorials and books available on this subject.

Nutrients

The key to improving plant growth is to ensure they have as many nutrients as possible to ensure maximum growth. This should be attainable by having the right feeding ratio combined with the correct BSA.

It is possible to increase the number of feed slightly in order to boost nutrient levels and achieve better and faster plant growth (especially for fruiting crops). More fish food means more ammonium, which leads to more available nitrogen and other micro and macronutrients.

Plants require a total of 13 macro and micronutrients to grow.

Primary macronutrients:

- Nitrogen (N)
- Phosphorus (P)
- Potassium (K)

Secondary Macronutrients:

- Calcium (Ca)
- Magnesium (Mg)
- Sulfur (S)

Micronutrients:

- Iron (Fe)
- Copper (Cu)
- Zinc (Zn)
- Manganese (Mn)
- Boron (B)
- Molybdenum (Mo)
- Chloride (Cl)

Out of these thirteen nutrients, ten of them can be supplied through the fish food. Only three need additional supplementation. These three are:

- Potassium (K)
- Calcium (Ca)
- Iron (Fe)

Calcium hydroxide and potassium hydroxide are already added to your system to increase the pH to 7. The only other nutrient you need to add is iron. You need to check the plant for the first sign of deficiencies. Kale is the first plant that will display iron deficiency. Having kale in your system is a good first indicator. Then add a chelated iron supplement to your system manually. We talked about iron deficiency in a previous chapter.

The Right Fish Food

Having a hobby setup or a commercial system has many advantages. You know that the produce is fresh and without pesticides.

But, do you know how the fish feed is produced?

Most commercial fish food is produced from what they call 'bycatch.' Bycatch is the result of unsustainable fishing techniques. It is the fish they didn't intend on catching or is a fish that is not worth much on the market.

Factories buy these fish at a low cost and turn them into fish food. The average food conversion rate to raise tilapia can range from 1.7 to 2. This means it takes 1.7 to 2 pounds of fish feed to raise one pound of fish. Doesn't look sustainable, does it?

You have the choice to choose for a more sustainable feed for your fish. A good source of organic feed is aquaorganic by the aquaponics source.

You can also minimize the need for fish food pellets. You can do this by growing duckweed. I will teach you how to grow duckweed later in this chapter.

If the fish food leaves a greasy film on top of your water, it might indicate that the fish food contains too many fats. Ether:

- Change out your fish food for a less fatty one with more protein.
- Redesign the return flow to your fish tank, so it breaks down the layer of fat that's on the surface.

Pollinating your plants

Flowering plants like strawberries or tomatoes need pollination. If you are growing outdoors, this won't be a problem because nature will do it for you. But if you are growing indoors or in a greenhouse, it is harder for insects to come in and pollinate the flowers.

I recommend going to a local beekeeper and ask him if you can use some bees (preferably mason bees). Another way is to pollinate by hand (using Qtips or the tip of your finger). Doing it manually, will obviously take more time and is not feasible with a big setup.

Airlift pump

With an airlift pump, you basically lift the water in a tank using an air pump or blower. I would only use an airlift pump on small hobby systems. Some numbers:

With a 45-watt air pump, you are able to lift the water 4 feet high (120cm) at a rate of 100 gallons (400 liters) per hour. The air pump is rated to deliver 4 gallons (15 liters) of air an hour. Here is how it works:

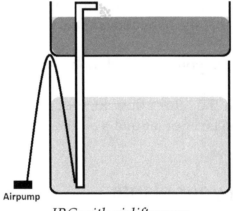

IBC with airlift pump

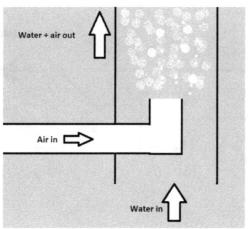

Close-up of the created airlift effect

Most of the time, it's more efficient to use a standard water pump in combination with a less powerful air pump to reach the same amount of dissolved oxygen.

Flow diversion

You are already aware of the fact that retention time in your solid's separator needs to be kept low. If your retention time is under 20 minutes, you have three options.

The first one was to install a bigger solids separator while the second option was to place another solids separator. Let's say you don't like these two options or are limited by space. Then there is a third option.

The third option is to redirect a part of the flow from your fish tank directly to your growbeds, or any other system you are using. This will skip the solids filtration, which will reduce the amount of water going through your separator.

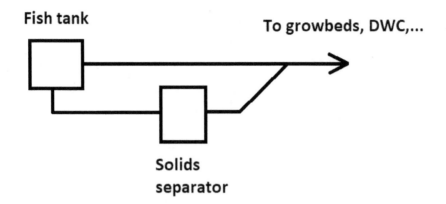

Diverting a part of the flow from the fish tank

The water we are going to divert needs to be as clean as possible. We want to minimize the number of solids that bypasses our solids separation. The cleanest water can be found just under the surface. Install an elbow that touches the water surface. Then, create a baffle or ring around it so the water on the surface won't enter the pipe. Install netting around it so fish can't enter the bypass.

You need to place a valve to control the flow through the bypass. The more water that travels through the bypass, the less water will go through the solids separator. You will have to fine-tune this in order for the solids to be sucked through the SLO. Reducing the diameter of the SLO will help improve suction. I advise the diameter to be no bigger than 2 inches when using this setup for an IBC.

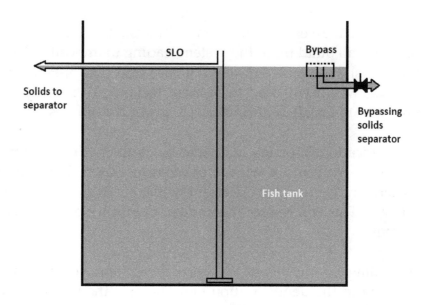

Bypassing solids separation

Denitrification

As you already know by now, the proven feeding rate for a high-density DWC aquaponics system is 60 to 100 grams of feed per square meter per day (60-100gr/m²/day).

Using this feeding ratio, the plants will have all the available nutrients required to grow except 3. Those three are iron, calcium, and potassium. Calcium and potassium are delivered by using a pH up mix in a 50-50 ratio. The only other nutrient you need to add manually is iron.

To make all the nutrients available to the plants, you are creating an excess of nitrogen (nitrates). Over time, these nitrates will build up in the system leading to unhealthy levels for the fish. Too much nitrates will also bring the N-P-K out of balance, which will lead to nutrient lockout. To remedy this, you need to install denitrification to lower the nitrates.

Denitrification happens in a separate tank **without** a lot of dissolved oxygen but with a lot of surface area. Denitrifying bacteria in the denitrification tank will convert the nitrate ions into gas. This will reduce the number of nitrates present in the system.

According to your measurements of the system, you can adjust the flow to the denitrification tank. Reduce the nitrates to an acceptable level (around 30ppm).

It's quite easy to make a denitrification tank. You need to create enough area for the bacteria to colonize using netting or any other bio media. You are basically creating a dead zone.

In small systems, this doesn't need to be big. If you see your nitrates at a higher level (+30ppm) while still feeding 60grams/m²/day, you would need to install a simple denitrification system.

It can be as simple as a 55-barrel cut in half and placed right after the solid's filtration (where dissolved oxygen is low).

Submerge netting in it and let the water overflow to the next part of your system. This tank will capture the fine solids that the solids filter didn't capture. If solids build-up, you need to clean it out. If nitrates are under 30ppm, remove the netting to bypass the denitrification process.

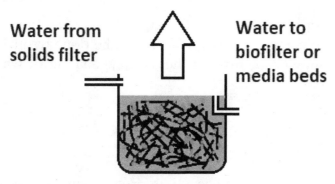

Nitrates dissolving

Water from
solids filter

Water to
biofilter or
media beds

A simple denitrification tank

Degassing

In the UVI system, they use a device called a degasser. It removes the toxic gasses (nitrogen gas and CO_2) the bacteria produce during the nitrification and denitrification process. Aerating the water will get rid of most of these toxic gasses.

In general, you don't need to use a degasser, only with high stocking levels. You will have enough oxygen going through the system in order for these gasses to disappear (evaporate), especially if you are using media beds.

The reason why the UVI system uses these is because they use a lot of denitrification. In denitrification, nitrogen gas is created. To get rid of these excessive gasses, they installed a degasser.

A degasser is more commonly used in commercial fish farms (aquaculture). Here they stock as many fish as they possibly can, but with that comes the need for an additional degasser.

If you see plant death in the first few feet of the floating rafts, you will have too many dissolved gasses in the system.

A degasser is simply a highly oxygenated area in your system where the gasses can escape. This can be done by installing a 'bakkie shower' or through heavy oxygenating of water in a tank.

Duckweed

Fish love duckweed. It has a high protein content and is full of nutrients for the fish. It will grow great in an aquaponics system. Duckweed loves slow-moving water and can double in size every 3 days. You can start growing duckweed in a separate container with a slow trickling flow. If you feed duckweed to your fish, they will require less commercial feed, which reduces your costs.

You can find duckweed in a pond nearby, or you can buy duckweed online on Amazon or eBay to get started.

In the following drawing, you can see a duckweed tank setup. The incoming water is directed to a net pot, so it doesn't disturb the surface of the water, which duckweed doesn't like.

On the outlet, there is another net pot in order for the duckweed to stay in the tank.

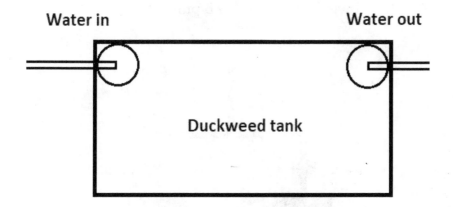

Duckweed tank setup top view

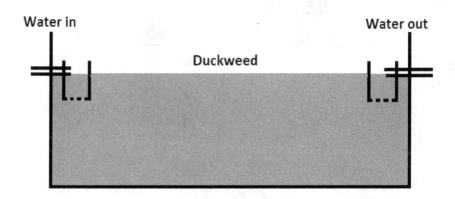

Duckweed tank side view

Backup pump

Arm yourself against the inevitable pump failure. This is crucial, especially in commercial setups. I still see many commercial setups without a backup pump. This is an accident waiting to happen! If the water in your fish tank isn't circulating, your fish can die very fast.

This is how I would set up an A/B pump system.

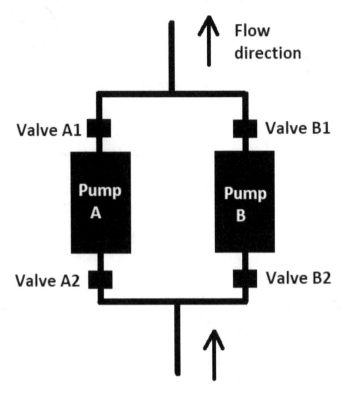

Backup inline pump

Pump A is running:

In normal operation, only pump A is running. If pump A is running, pump B is turned off. Valves A1, A2, and B1 are open. B2 is closed.

Why is valve B1 open?
You should never block in a pump completely. If you would block in pump B by closing B1 and B2, the pressure in the pump can build up. If the water inside pump B is heated by sunlight or another heat source, the water will expand, and the pump's seals will break.

Never block in a pump!

Why do you close valve B1 instead of closing B2?
When you accidentally turn on pump B without noticing, you create a vacuum in pump B. This is also known as cavitation, which will damage the pump. Centrifugal pumps can pump water against the blocked-in pressure side of the pump without damaging themselves.

An even better setup would be to have both pumps A and B running at 50% of their speed. When pump A fails, the water is still cycling for 50%. When you check the system and notice the pump failure, you can switch pump B to 100%. Block in pump A by closing valves A1 and A2 and replace the broken pump. This will cost more because you need to run frequency drives.

Venturi

Using a venturi is a good method of oxygenating the water before it returns to the fish tank. You need to have pressurized water for the venturi to work properly.

How it works:

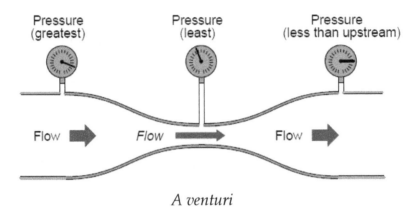

A venturi

A venturi works by creating a narrow restriction for the water to go through. The water will enter the venturi with a low flow rate but at high pressure. Right after the water passes the restriction, there is suction created (low-pressure point) by the expanding water after the restriction.

This suction will allow the air to enter and mix in with the water. The end result is water at a lower pressure mixed with air. There will be an arrow on the venturi to indicate the flow direction.

There are two kinds of venturi's you can use:

- Commercial venturi

A commercial venturi

- DIY venturi

People have come up with a DIY venturi. I'm not a fan of these because the output is rather disappointing. But if you are up for a challenge, you can make one yourself.

There are many options to make one yourself. I'm going to show you the most used method:

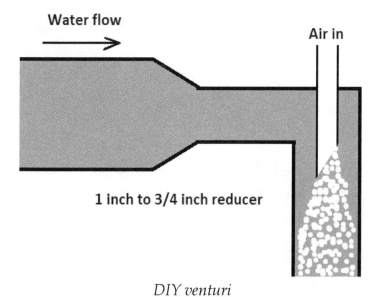

DIY venturi

The water flow comes in at high pressure (after the pump). It goes through 1-inch piping, which is reduced to ¾ of an inch. At the top of the elbow, there is a hole drilled to insert a small flexible hose. The rubber hose is cut at a 45-degree angle to maximize the air input.

A 1 inch to ¾ inch reducer was used with a pump that delivers 900gph with great results.

The smaller the bubbles, the better the aeration of the water. That's why purchasing a professional venturi is the way to go. They are specially designed to maximize aeration. A small ¼inch venturi will cost you around $15 on Amazon.

Heating

If winter gets cold, your fish might not turn out as much ammonium as you want because their metabolism slows down. Your fish might even die when it gets too cold. That's why you should heat the water in your system.

Here are a few things you can do to keep the temperature from dropping:

- Use a greenhouse.
- Insulate your fish tank.
- Insulate growbeds or DWC.

If you have applied the previous methods, but the water is still getting too cold, you can use the following methods:

- Electrical heating element.

An electrical heating element should only be relied on in an emergency but could work in a small system. The cost of running an electrical heating element in your fish tank can become expensive very quickly! You can get electrical pond heaters online or from your fish store.

The bigger your water mass, the longer it will take for your temperature to rise. Choosing a higher wattage heater will reduce the time it takes to heat the water. You can place the heating element directly in your fish tank because they will have a heat guard around them so fish won't get burned.

Most of these heaters will come with a built-in thermostat, which will shut off when the desired temperature is reached.

- Propane or natural gas heater.

A more economical method of heating is to use a water heater that works on propane. This system could be used in a commercial setup because it doesn't cost that much to buy a heater, and it is reliable. It's more complex to install such a system for your backyard system and is probably not worth the upfront investment. For commercial farms, this is very cost-effective.

- Solar PEX heater.

An option that's very popular amongst the DIY community is using a solar water heater using PEX (food grade) flexible 1-inch piping. The PEX piping is rolled up in a coil. The coil is enclosed in a wooden frame and sometimes covered with plexiglass. Everything is painted black to increase heat absorption from the sun.

You can place the solar heater right after your pump or use a split flow from the sump pump to your fish tank and solar heater. Desertsun02 on YouTube has done a great job of explaining how he made his own solar PEX heater. You can watch the video where he explains how he made it.

Desertsun02's video on how to make a solar pex heater

- Woodstove heating

Another method of heating the water is using a wood stove. Make a copper coil and put it in the enclosed firebox. Make sure that there is always running water through the copper pipe. You can use a split-flow from the sump or use a separate loop with a separate pump.

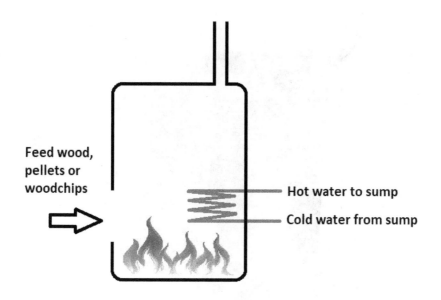

Using a wood stove for heating water

You can go to your local sawmill and ask if they have wood scraps or sawdust. You can even make your own pellets from this sawdust.

- Compost pile heating

A low-cost technique to heat your water is to use flexible piping and run it through a pile of compost. Have you ever put your hands inside of compost? If not, you will be surprised by how much heat it generates!

Straw
Leaves
Chicken Manure
Lawn Clippings
Straw
Lawn Clippings

Manure

Straw

Newspaper
Manure

An easy DIY water heater

You can go as big as you want with this. Use a split flow from the sump or install a separate pump where you are circulating the water in a separate loop.

Beware!
When heating up water, make sure there are no enclosed spaces in the tubing. When the water heats up, the pressure will increase, and it can burst. Install an emergency pressure release valve in an enclosed heating system or leave at least one end open to release pressure build-up.

Tip
Try to return the hot water to the sump instead of the fish tank. Hot water directly into the fish tank might burn or stress the fish when they swim near it. Instead, allow it to get mixed in with the colder water in your sump.

If you don't use a sump, a good idea is to let it flow to your solid's separator. This way, the water gets mixed in with the colder water. Do not put the hot water directly in your growbeds or any other planting/bacterial area.

Cooling

Doing the opposite might be necessary during the summer.

First of all, if you are growing in a greenhouse, installing vents and fans that create airflow in and out of your greenhouse would be the first step. Consider adding shade cloth to the greenhouse to block out the sun.

Here are some other options if forced airflow isn't enough:

- Change out water from the system.

This should be used in an emergency situation. In large commercial scale operations, this wouldn't be a viable option. You basically drain the water and introduce colder water from the tap or from a rainwater collection sump. Don't exchange all the water because the fish, plants, and bacteria don't like sudden drops in temperature. The nutrients that are dissolved in the water will flow to your drain.

- Evaporate cooler.

An evaporate cooler or cooling wall is an easy and cost-effective solution to cool down a greenhouse. It's a wall where water drips down on a wall of media. The air will be pulled in by the fans on the opposite side of the greenhouse. The outside air will enter the greenhouse and be cooled by the evaporation of the water. Cooling the greenhouse will cool down the water for your fish and plants.

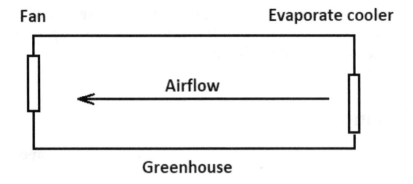

Fan

Evaporate cooler

Airflow

Greenhouse

The placement of an evaporate cooler

In this design, there would be two fans at the left of the greenhouse pulling air from the greenhouse to the outside. There would be one evaporate cooler on the other side of the greenhouse.

- Fan 1 kicks in when the temperature reaches 70 degrees.
- Fan 2 kicks in when the temperature reaches 75 degrees.
- The evaporate cooler will kick in when the temperature reaches 80 degrees.

Many people make an evaporative cooler by themselves because they are surprisingly easy to make. You would have to buy the cooling media from specialized stores.

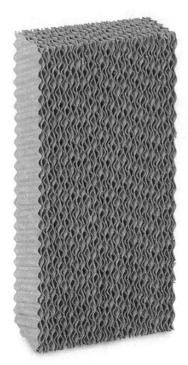

The media that is used in an evaporate cooler

Here is a setup you can use:

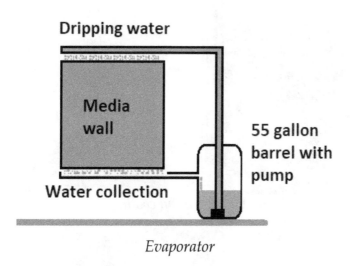

Evaporator

The evaporator cooler works well in dry climates. It wouldn't work as well in a humid climate. Watch the reservoir because it drains fast. You can install a float switch to auto top up the water in the barrel and a thermostat to start the pump.

Install bug netting in front of the cooler and an enclosure so you can close it down from the outside during the colder months of the year.

- Underground loop.

If you are not using a greenhouse, there is another way to cool your water during summer. You can use a separate loop with a pump that runs at least three feet underground. Connect your pump and let it exchange the heat of the water with the cooler earth. Turn off the pump manually if the desired temperature is reached.

You can install an additional thermostat to make this process automated.

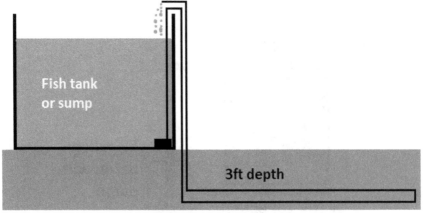

Underground cooling

System isolation

We already learned that different plants like different electrical conductivity levels (EC's). For example, lettuce needs around 1 EC, while tomatoes need between 2 and 5 EC.

Lettuce requires fewer nutrients than tomatoes. But planting lettuce and tomatoes together is not efficient. Lettuce doesn't like high EC, and tomatoes don't grow as well in low EC.

The primary minerals that make up EC are:

- N: Nitrogen
- P: Phosphorous
- K: Potassium

Vegetative plants like lots of nitrogen but don't need much potassium. The potassium will be supplied by the pH up formula I talked about earlier.

It might be a good idea to create two separate systems, one for vegetative plants and one for fruiting plants so you can create the optimal environment for each.

Let's say you have a vegetative system that requires an EC of one. You can keep the EC around one when you reduce feeding rates (to a minimum of 60grams/m²/day). After a while, the pH drops because of the nitrification, and you add the pH up formula. Potassium gets introduced in the system (by the pH up formula), and vegetating plants use if for their water uptake. The lettuce is happy in its environment and grows quickly.

Fruiting plants, on the other hand, require more potassium. The fish feed has potassium in it, but it's required by the fish to grow. This creates a potassium deficiency for fruiting plants. Yes, you would pH adjust it with the pH up formula, but that's probably not enough for big systems. You would need to supplement additional potassium in the system for these fruits to become big.

The main advantage of system isolation is that you are creating the optimal growing environment for the plants.

Calculating a commercial system

In this chapter, I'm going to calculate a commercial system based on plant growth. Plant growth will be the most profitable and the limiting factor in your installation because of space.

This is a calculation for a commercial deep-water culture system. The feeding ratios used will be for a DWC system.

Let's get started!

Suppose you want to grow 1000 heads of lettuce each week.

You can grow 16 heads of lettuce in one square meter, and the lettuce will be in the seedling nursery for one week and on the floating rafts for 4 weeks.

Knowing this, you can calculate how much growing space you need.

$$4\ weeks\ x\ 1000\ heads = 4000\ heads\ of\ lettuce$$

$$\frac{4000\ heads\ of\ lettuce}{16\ heads\ per\ square\ meter} = 250\ m^2\ of\ raft\ area$$

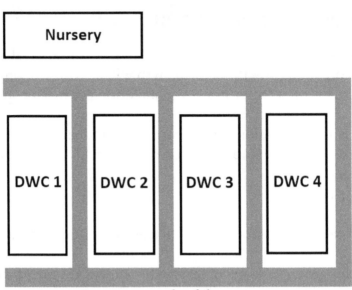

Layout example of the system

Now you need to choose your preferred feeding ratio.

If you make money on the fish, you should choose for a high-density system, which will be 60-100 grams of feed per square meter per day.

If you don't make money on the fish, you need to use a low-density system and use 16 grams of feed per square meter per day.

In this example, I'm going to make money from the fish, so I choose to use 80 grams per square meter of feed per day.

Now calculate the amount of fish feed needed per day for 250m².

$$80 \; grams \; x \; 250m^2 = 20,000 \; grams \; of \; feed \; per \; day$$

Now, calculate the feed input per year:

$$20,000 \; x \; 365 = 7,300,000 \; grams$$

Convert grams to pounds:

$$\frac{7,300,000 \; grams}{454} = 16,079 \; pounds \; of \; feed \; per \; year$$

Now, see how much pounds of fish you are going to have when you feed 16,079 pounds of fish feed in a year while knowing the feed conversion rate for tilapia is 2.

$$\frac{16,079 \; pounds}{2} = 8,039 \; pounds \; of \; fish \; in \; one \; year$$

Tilapia takes 6 months, 24 weeks, or 182 days before they reach one pound in weight after they are bought as fingerlings (2 months old).

I bought fish from the hatchery at a weight of 0.05 pounds per fish. I will sell these fish to local restaurants, and they would like to work with a one-pound fish.

The fish we have in the system will, therefore, gain the weight of:

$$1 \; pound - 0.05 \; pound = 0.95 \; pound \; of \; weight \; gain$$

The total amount of fish weight gain per year will be:

$$\frac{8,039 \; pound \; of \; fish}{0.95} = 8,462 \; pounds \; at \; harvest$$

I decide I want to use staggered fish production and use 6 tanks. This is to have consistent fish sales and, more importantly, a stable nutrient supply for the plants.

$$\frac{182\ days}{6\ tanks} = 30.33\ days\ between\ harvests$$

This means we will have:

$$\frac{365\ days}{30.33\ days} = 12\ harvests\ per\ year$$

Next, we calculate the weight of the fish that we will harvest every 30 days. We do this by taking the total amount of fish production per year and divide it by the number of harvests we have each year.

$$\frac{8,462\ pounds}{12\ harvests}\ 705\ pounds\ of\ fish\ each\ harvest$$

Then divide this amount by the weight of the fish at harvest.

$$\frac{705\ pounds\ of\ fish}{1\ pound\ fish} = 705\ fish\ per\ harvest$$

We can sell 705 fish at the market with a total weight of 705 pounds total each month. You will need to round these numbers down to account for fish deaths.

Now we need to calculate how big the fish tank needs to be to house these fish. If we use tilapia, we know that they do well at a stocking density of one pound per 2 to 3 gallons of water.

We would need:

$$705\ one\ pound\ fish\ x\ 2\ gallons\ per\ pound = 1,410\ gallons$$

Using 6 – 1500 gallon tanks would be ideal because there needs to be a brim at the top for the fish not to jump out, netting on top of the tank is also advised. The maximum amount of fish in the system will be:

$$705 \; fish \; x \; 6 \; tanks = 4{,}230 \; fish$$

An overview of the system:
- It will produce 1000 heads of lettuce each week.
- It will produce 705 pounds of fish every month.
- It needs 16,079 pounds of feed each year.
- It's a high-density system.

$$\frac{4{,}230 \; pounds \; of \; fish}{2{,}690 ft^2} = 1.57$$

Calculating a hobby system

For the hobby system, I'm going to use growbeds filled with hydroton. I will be using beds made from an IBC and an IBC tote for the fish.

Because it's a backyard system, you are not going to grow one kind of crop. You might be planting lettuce, basil, kale, or any other plant that is suitable for aquaponics.

Let's say you want to build a system that has 36ft² of growbed area. That's exactly 3 cut IBC's. You will fill them up with 12 inches of hydroton and one inch of dry media on top. This system is drawn in the next chapter, the advanced IBC setup.

The feeding ratio for growbeds is 15 to 40 grams per square meter per day.

Feeding 15 grams will not allow you to grow fruiting crops, while 40 grams will increase nutrient availability to the plants. Fruiting crops should only be added after the system is running for a few months.

$$\frac{36ft^2}{10.76} = 3.34m^2$$

I choose 40 grams per square meter per day.

$$40 \ grams \ x \ 3.34m^2 = 133.6 \ grams \ of \ feed \ per \ day$$

How much fish feed do you need in one year?

$$133.6 \ x \ 365 = 48,764 \ grams \ of \ feed \ per \ year$$

Convert to pounds:

$$\frac{48,764 \ grams}{454} = 107.4 \ pounds \ of \ feed \ input \ per \ year$$

Next, figure out the food conversion rate (FCR) for the fish you intend to use. For tilapia, this is 2.

$$\frac{107.4 \ pounds}{2} = 53.7 \ pounds \ of \ fish \ gain \ per \ year$$

Tilapia takes 6 months, 24 weeks, or 182 days before they reach one pound in weight after they are bought as fingerlings (2 months old). I bought fish from the hatchery at a weight of 0.05 pounds per fish.

I will take the fish out of the system when they reach one pound.

The fish we have in the system will gain a weight of:

$$1 \; pound - 0.05 \; pound = 0.95 \; pound$$

The total amount of fish production per year will be:

$$\frac{53.7 \; pounds}{0.95 \; pound} = 56.5 \; pounds$$

Harvesting twice a year makes sense because it takes 6 months for the tilapia to grow to one pound (12 months/6 months).

$$\frac{56 \; pounds \; of \; fish}{2 \; harvests} = 28 \; fish$$

This stocking density is close to the optimal feeding ratio for tilapia. I have talked about the optimal feeding ratio in the 'step by step guide' chapter earlier in the book.

5 grams per day on average, is the optimal feeding rate for tilapia.

$$\frac{133 \; grams \; of \; feed \; per \; day}{5 \; grams} = 26.6 \; fish$$

Now you need to check if your growbeds can mineralize the solids in the system without additional solids filtration. We use the ratio of 1 pound of fish per square feet (system density of 1). We have a system with 28 pounds of fish (max capacity) and 36ft² of growing area.

Remember the formula to figure out system density?

$$Density = \frac{Fish \; in \; pounds}{Grow \; area \; in \; ft^2}$$

$$\frac{28 \; pounds \; of \; fish}{36 ft^2} = 0.77$$

In growbeds, you should aim for a density under one. This is in between a low-density system (0.3) and a high-density system (1.5). A density under one will not require solids filtration as the media beds are big enough to handle the solids without having to clean them out (if solids are distributed evenly across the surface).

With this hobby system, you will only have one tank. If you are using one tank, you are decreasing the nutrient availability throughout the year. Your plants won't have as many nutrients during the restocking phase. The nutrient availability for your plants will look something like this:

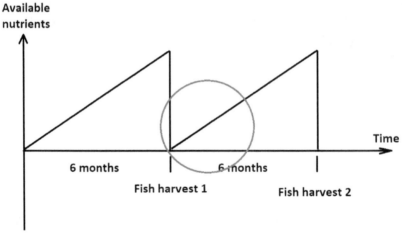

Nutrient availability when using one fish tank

The circle indicates low nutrients in the system just after the fish are harvested. This is not optimal, and that's why commercial systems use multiple fish tanks.

Because we only use one fish tank, I advise to divide the tank in half and use netting to separate the fish from each other. This can be done by installing a wooden frame with the netting attached to it, which you can move in the IBC when the fish get bigger. The nutrients in the system will now look like this: (top line)

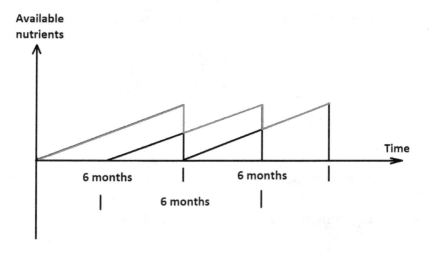

The nutrients are more balanced using this stocking system

If you are using this stocking system, you would only need to stock half the fish in the beginning and add the other half after 3 months. You are basically mimicking using two fish tanks. This is called staggered production.

$$\frac{182\ days}{2\ tanks} = 91\ days\ or\ 3\ months\ between\ harvest$$

This means we will have:

$$\frac{365\ days}{91\ days} = 4\ harvests\ each\ year$$

Next, we calculate the weight of the fish that we will harvest every 91 days. We do this by taking the total amount of fish production per year and divide it by the number of harvests we have each year.

$$\frac{56.5 \; pounds \; of \; fish \; per \; year}{4 \; harvests} = 14.125 \; pounds \; of \; fish$$

Then divide this amount by the weight of the fish at harvest.

$$\frac{14.125 \; pounds \; of \; fish}{1 \; pound \; fish} = 14 \; fish$$

You can harvest 14 fish with a total weight of 14 pounds four times a year.

Now we need to calculate how big the fish tank needs to be to house these fish. If we use tilapia, we know that they do well at a stocking density at one pound per 2 gallons of water.

Now, because we are using two different sizes of fish in one tank, we need to factor these in. When the first batch is harvested, the other ones are 3 months old (around half their adult weight).

$$14 \; pounds + 7 \; pounds = 21 \; pounds \; of \; fish$$

21 pounds of fish in the IBC tote, at most, right before harvest.

For tilapia, we need:

$$21 \; pounds \; x \; 2 \; gallons \; per \; pound = 42 \; gallons$$

If you are using trout, you will need:

$$21 \; pounds \; x \; 8 \; gallons \; per \; pound = 168 \; gallons$$

System designs

I will explain a few popular systems:

- One-barrel system
- Two barrels system
- Vertical rack
- Cut and flip
- Advanced IBC setup
- Media bed with DWC
- Vertical towers
- Dutch buckets
- Commercial setup

One-barrel system

The one-barrel system is the easiest aquaponics setup while still having some growing space. This would be a great demo setup for a school or a small project to show how aquaponics works.

Basically, you take a 55-gallon drum and cut it in half approximately 14 inches from the top. You will then have to install a siphon of your choice and add media to the top part. The top will be flipped over and put on top of the bottom of the barrel. The bottom of the barrel will be your fish tank.

A one-barrel system is just a smaller version of the more common cut and flip IBC setup.

A one-barrel aquaponics system (image from lonesomecreekranch)

Two-barrel system

A two-barrel system uses one 55 gallon barrel as the fish tank. The fish tank can be either standing or laying down. You can choose what works best for you. The other barrel is cut in half lengthwise and filled with media. Each half-barrel uses a siphon to return the water back to the fish barrel.

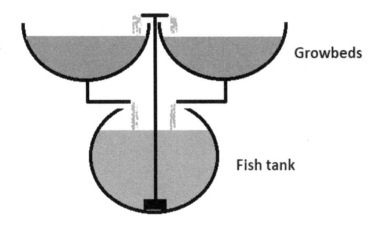

A two-barrel system

Alternatively, you can connect the growbeds together and install an external siphon. This is done in systems that have small growbeds, and adding one siphon in each bed would take up a lot of space. Make sure the external siphon is level with the growbeds as this will decide the flood level.

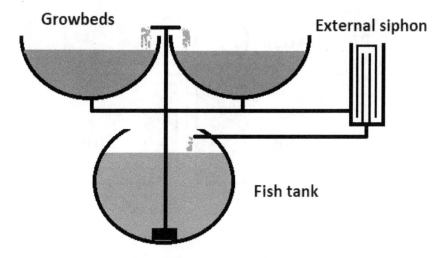

Growbeds with an external siphon

Vertical rack

This is a borrowed setup from hydroponics. If you are growing indoors, this might be a good setup for you. Growing indoors might come with space limitations. Keeping this in mind, we are using a biofilter instead of a growbed. This design is basically a vertical DWC system. Limit the depth to a maximum of 5 inches to reduce the weight.

Water flows down by gravity. You need to adjust the split flow from the sump to make sure there is enough water flow to the DWC beds. The sump can also be placed under the grow rack.

As for the lights, I suggest using 3 x 4ft T5 fluorescents at a kelvin rating of 6500K at each level. For a total of 9 T5 lights.

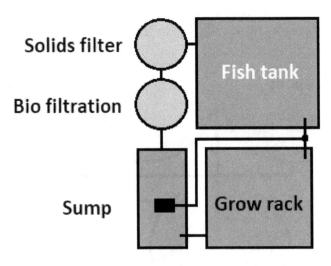

The vertical grow rack top view

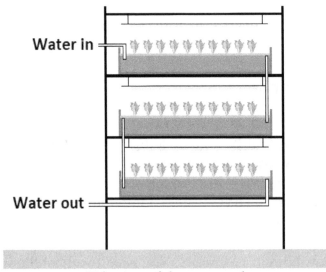

Side view of the grow rack

Cut and Flip

This is the most basic system; it's geared towards beginners. It is a basic IBC setup that uses one IBC that's cut approximately 15 inches from the top. Then it's flipped to create a fish tank, and a grow bed on top of each other.

The fish tank has an approximate volume of 150 gallons, and the grow bed should be 15 inches high. 12 inches of the grow bed should be covered with river rock (or another suitable media) that are getting submerged with the flood cycle. 1 inch of dry rock should be added above the 12 inches of river rock. This prevents algae from forming and is used to weight down clay pebbles. It also decreases the evaporation from the system.

A siphon of your choice is added in the grow bed to allow the flood and drain cycle to work. All the water in the fish tank should cycle once every hour.

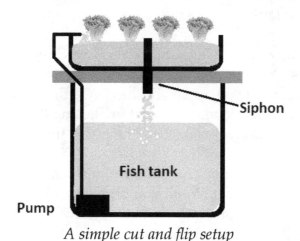

A simple cut and flip setup

Be aware that the water level in the fish tank will drop once you start to fill the media bed. Select the right pump when you take the head height into consideration.

Advanced IBC setup

The grow bed technique is still being used, but there are more components to the system. The grow beds are next to each other, and the sump tank is between the fish tank and the grow beds.

There is a split flow from the pump in the sump tank to the fish tank and grow beds. In this system, there should be three ball valves immediately before the water goes into the grow beds.

By doing this, the flow is equally distributed to the grow beds. You should also add a ball valve right after the T piece that goes back to your fish tank. This way, you can control the flow to your fish tank and adjust it accordingly.

The SLO (solids lifting overflow) needs to be done correctly like discussed in this book. Otherwise, you are at risk of creating a siphon during an electricity outage and suck all the water out of your fish tank.

Note that the water in the sump is almost as high as the ground level. This prevents the sump from being pushed up by the groundwater. The edges should be above the surface in order for flood water or debris not to get in. Raising the water level in the sump also decreases the head height of the pump.

Having a split flow means you are more adaptable to future changes to the system. When you decide to add dutch buckets, you can add a line of dutch buckets or vertical towers to it.

Isolation becomes easier when using a split flow. You can decide to do maintenance on the fish tank while the water is still cycling in the growbeds or vice-versa.

You will need to oversize your pump if you are using a split flow. If you are going to use a 50-50 split-flow, you have to double the flow of the pump.

You do not need to install a split flow if you want to keep the size of the pump as low as possible. Systems can work perfectly without a split flow.

System with split-flow

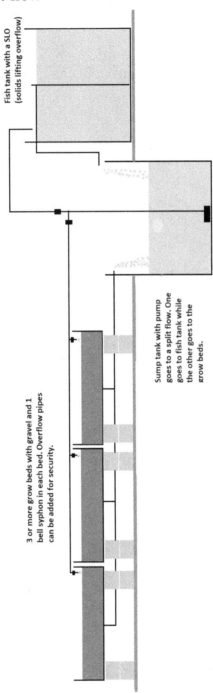

Fish tank with a SLO
(solids lifting overflow)

Sump tank with pump goes to a split flow. One goes to fish tank while the other goes to the grow beds.

3 or more grow beds with gravel and 1 bell syphon in each bed. Overflow pipes can be added for security.

System without split-flow

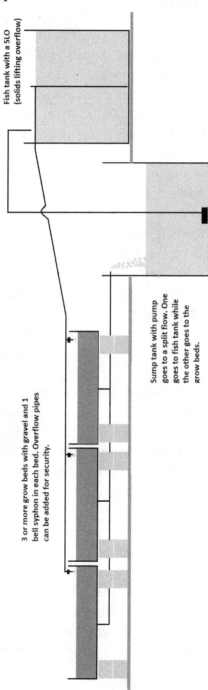

Fish tank with a SLO (solids lifting overflow)

3 or more grow beds with gravel and 1 bell syphon in each bed. Overflow pipes can be added for security.

Sump tank with pump goes to a split flow. One goes to fish tank while the other goes to the grow beds.

DWC with media beds

The following setup is a deep-water culture system combined with a media bed. Now, why would you choose a media bed in combination with a DWC system?

To cut costs on biofiltration and to create additional mineralization and growing space. You need to calculate how much bio-media you need in your growbeds in order to convert all the ammonia to nitrates for your DWC system. You can do this by using the chapter 'calculating BSA' in this book.

Depending on how big you are going to make this setup, you still need additional solids filtration. The solids you are capturing should be sent over to an additional mineralization tank. The growbeds are basically fine solids capturing filters but should not be relied on to capture all the solids. Adding worms to the media bed is essential to break down these fine solids.

As a benefit, you can plant herbs or any other plant that likes media beds instead of a DWC system. You don't need a sump tank for this setup. The DWC troughs will act as the sump. When water evaporates, the water level in the troughs (sump) will lower. Your rafts will lower as a result. Having a float switch to top up the water automatically can automate the task.

A mineralization tank is added to the system to convert all the fish waste into useful nutrients for the plants.

It's important not to make your media beds too big. It's better to have smaller media beds than larger ones because they are easier to isolate. When you want to do maintenance on one media bed, you are not phasing out a big part of your bacteria.

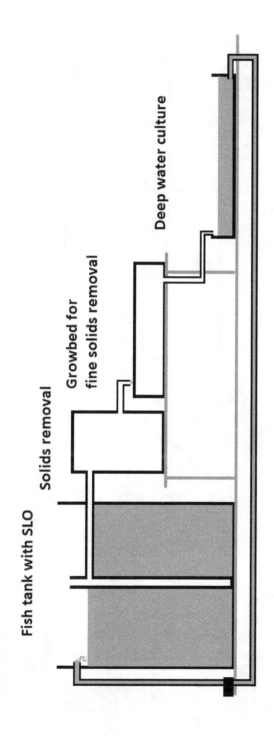

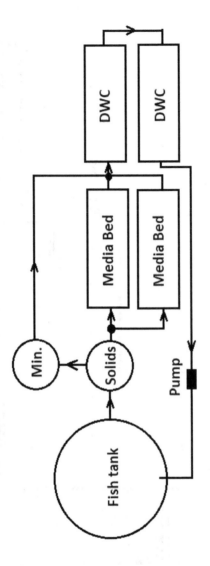

Note that the return line from the DWC is not an overflow. If the water level lowers, the pump would be running dry. That's why the pump inlet is placed at the bottom of the DWC. If the water level drops, the pump still has water to return to the fish tank.

Vertical towers

Vertical towers are becoming quite popular because they save space. The downside to vertical towers is that there is not enough surface area for the bacteria. You need a biofilter or a media bed like the DWC with grow beds.

For this example, I'm going to use a biofilter. Again, you will need to calculate the BSA you need using the chapter 'calculating BSA.'

The setup uses the sump tank as a central point in the system. The reason for returning everything to the sump tank is because it's easy to isolate parts of the system. There is an option to return the water from the solids filter to the sump if needed.

The pump has a split flow from the sump to the grow towers. This way, the flow rate to the towers can be adjusted accordingly. Each tower has a separate valve so the towers can be disconnected from the system. It looks like this:

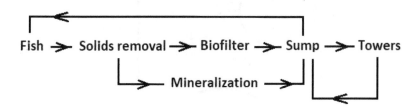

Tower setup with biofilter

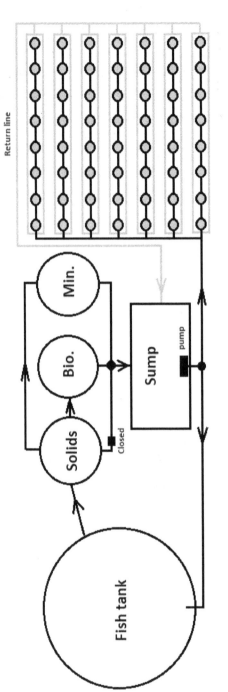

Return line

Vertical towers

Min.

Bio.

Solids

Closed

Sump

pump

Fish tank

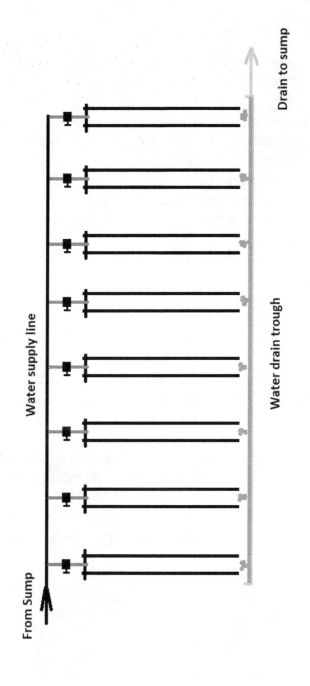

Dutch buckets

Another system that is widely used. Dutch buckets are mainly used for growing tomatoes and peppers.

Tomatoes, peppers, and other fruiting plants require a high amount of nutrients to produce fruit. In order to give them these nutrients, we need a good bacteria colony and a high feeding rate ($60grams/m^2/day$ at least). The media in the buckets won't be enough to supply a great amount of nitrification. That's why you should add a media bed or a biofilter.

I make the dutch buckets separate from the system so you can isolate them if needed. You need to make sure you have enough BSA for the dutch buckets. It's better to have fewer plants with some nutrients leftover than a lot of plants, which all have to share a tiny amount of nutrients. Using dutch buckets would be a great addition to an already existing media bed system. If you notice you have quite some nitrates in your system (5+), you can expand to fruiting crops.

I have made this system plug and play so you can add the dutch buckets later on. You can add a mineralization tank to it if you want.

You can use a split-flow on this setup if you want to.

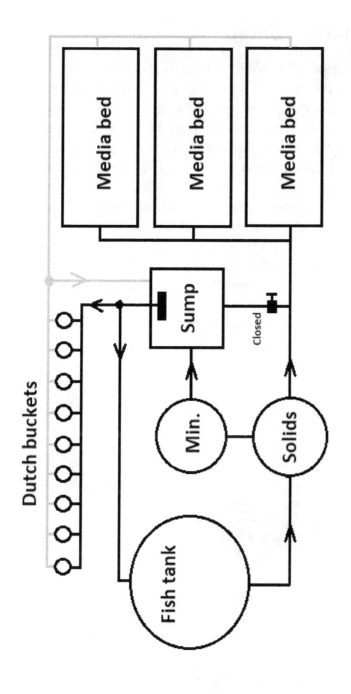

Commercial Setup

The University of the Virgin Islands (UVI) has created a proven and tested method of raising fish and plants together. I wanted to share their design with you because if you go commercial, then the numbers are critical. They have published a PDF with all the information, yields, and profits from running with basil, romaine lettuce, and okra combined with red and Nile tilapia

They run the system using only 3 horsepower, which equates to 2.23 kilowatts. If they run this system 24/7, they would consume 53.5k watts/hour in one day. If the energy cost per kilowatt-hour is $0.12, that will make it $6.42 in energy costs per day, $45 per week, or $2337 per year. Not bad.

With a commercial aquaponics setup, labor cost and fish feed are the highest. Making an almost maintenance-free system is the top priority.

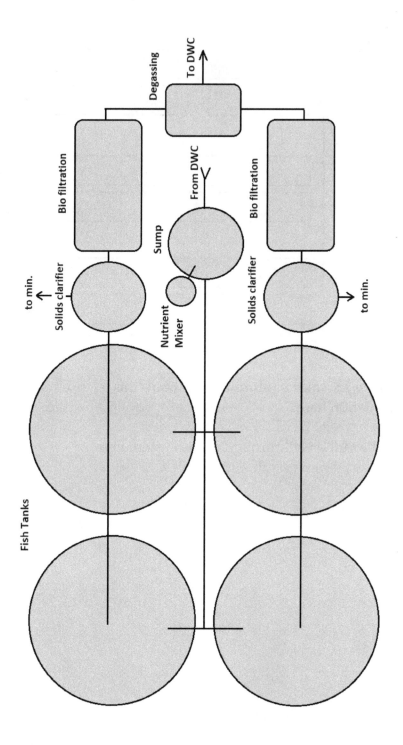

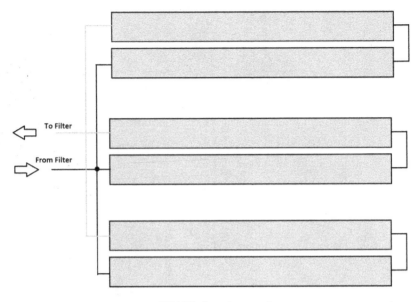

DWC floating rafts

If you want more information about this setup, visit their presentation here: https://www.howtoaquaponic.com/uvi

And the video walkthrough of the system here:
https://www.howtoaquaponic.com/uvi-video

Summing Up Aquaponics

If you're experimenting with aquaponics, then there are some essential things that you must remember and apply to your own setup:

Design
You must take the time to think about your design. It's essential to choose the right location for both the fish and the grow beds. Easy access, shade for your fish, and a controllable environment will make a huge difference to the success of your new system. Taking the time to plan will allow you to achieve success on the first attempt.

Patience
It is essential that you have patience when creating the system. This means waiting for the nitrifying bacteria to colonize the media. Having patience will reward you in the long run.

Experiment
It is also important to be prepared to experiment with different possibilities. Whether you want to try different fish, different plants or even change the growing media; experimenting by changing small details can make a huge difference to the success of your system.

But as always, it is essential to change things one bit at a time and document everything you do. This will ensure you can work out what really works for your system and what doesn't.

Monitor

Monitoring water quality is essential to ensure your plants and fish are happy together with the best possible conditions to grow in. You need to test the following and monitor the results carefully.

- **Water pH** – Test once a week after the cycling of your system. You're looking for values between 6.5 and 7.5.

- **Water hardness (GH)** – Any reading between 50ppm and 100ppm is good. Well water is 'harder water;' tropical fish don't like hard water. Water hardness is a combination of calcium and magnesium. If the water hardness is too high, some nutrients might get locked out. Having a water hardness of 80 is recommended. Harder water is typically more alkaline, thus higher pH.

- **Alkalinity (KG)** – Alkalinity resists a change in pH. Having a high level of alkalinity will make it harder for your system to drop in pH. You should aim for a minimum of 80ppm. Alkaline (high pH) and alkalinity are not the same. You can test GH and KG very cheaply using the following test kit:

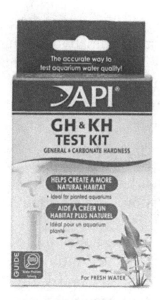

HG and KG test kit

- **Dissolved Oxygen levels –** If fish are gasping for air at the surface, there is a problem. If the temperature rises, the metabolism of the fish will rise, and dissolved oxygen levels in the water will drop. It's important to monitor the behavior of your fish when the temperature rises. If they gasp for air, add more aeration and check for decaying fish food or dead fish in your tank. Tilapia is adapted to warm water and will slow down metabolism and air consumption. Aim for 5ppm and 10ppm for trout. Plants need oxygen too, failing to supply them with oxygen will lead to root rot.

- **Ammonium –** 0ppm before feeding is ideal. This should be checked daily when establishing your system. Later on, when your system is mature, you can check this once a week. Consult the table earlier in this book to check for the maximum levels at specific temperatures and pH levels.

- **Nitrites** – ideally, this would be zero. Don't let it go higher than 0.5ppm. If it goes higher, you need to reduce feeding. High nitrites mean no Nitrobacter bacteria to convert nitrites to nitrates. Stop feeding the fish until nitrites are down again, and the bacteria have populated your system.

- **Nitrate** – Anything up to 30ppm is okay. If you have a system that has 30ppm+, means you need to introduce denitrification. Aim for a minimum of 5ppm.

  In a recirculating aquaculture system (RAS), there was a test done on what kind of impact nitrates have on feed conversion, stress, and growth rate by Nile tilapia. It turns out that growth was negatively affected when it went above 500ppm.

- **Iron deficiency** – If new leaves are turning yellow, you should do an iron test. If pH is above 7.5, your plants might not be able to take up iron efficiently. if levels are low, you may want to test daily until they are correct again. You're looking for a range between 2 and 3ppm. Anything below 1.5ppm will show as yellow leaves on your plants. Some plants will show this before others.

- **Sulfur** – You're aiming for levels below 60ppm, a monthly test should be enough.

- **Zinc** – Higher than .05ppm is toxic to your fish. Ideally, check this once a week at the beginning.

Cheat Sheet

60-100g/m² of raft area in DWC
15-40g/m² in growbeds
15-25g/m² for NFT

$$Total\ BSA = System\ BSA + Media\ BSA$$

$$Media\ BSA = Volume\ of\ grow\ bed\ in\ ft^3 x\ SSA$$

- Sand – 270 ft²/ft³
- ¾ inch crushed granite – 45-60 ft²/ft³
- Expanded clay (hydroton) – 70 ft²/ft³
- Lava rock – 85 ft²/ft³
- Pea gravel – 85 ft²/ft³
- River rock – 20 ft²/ft³
- Bio tube media – 125 ft²/ft³
- White Matala filter media – 171 ft²/ft³
- Blue Matala filter media – 124 ft²/ft³
- Kaldnes (K1) – 250 ft²/ft³
- Zip grow matrix media – 290 ft²/ft³
- Root area of lettuce is 10ft²/ft²

50ft² of BSA for every pound of fish.

$$Amount\ of\ fish\ in\ pounds = \frac{Total\ BSA}{50ft^2}$$

- Low-density = 0.3
- High-density = 1.5
- Grow bed density = 1

$$System\ density = \frac{Fish\ in\ pounds}{Grow\ area\ in\ ft^2}$$

$$Fish\ in\ pounds = Density\ x\ Grow\ area\ in\ ft^2$$

$$Grow\ area\ in\ ft^2 = \frac{Fish\ in\ pounds}{Density}$$

Useful Resources

Forums

- backyardaquaponics.com/forum
- diyaquaponics.com/forum
- aquaponicsnation.com/forums

YouTube Channels

- Bright Agrotech
- Rob Bob's Aquaponics & Backyard Farm
- Murray Hallam Aquaponics
- Ponic Wars (Channel discontinued but still useful)

Useful Websites

- howtoaquaponic.com
- friendlyaquaponics.com
- backyardaquaponics.com
- aquaponicsnation.com
- blog.zipgrow.com

Proven system (University of the Virgin Islands):
https://www.uvi.edu/files/documents/Research_and_Public_
Service/WRRI/UVIAquaponicSystem.pdf

Endnote

It was a pleasure writing this book.

You can do as you please with this book, apply this information to create a successful aquaponics system, or pass this book to a friend who might be interested in trying it out.

Seeing people succeed with their aquaponics system is always great to see. When you do decide to make a system but have some questions, do not hesitate to contact me on my email or through my website.

Enjoy growing!
Nick

Alphabetical Index

AC: Alternating current which you have coming out of any house socket.
aerobic: A zone with a lot of dissolved oxygen
anaerobic: A zone without a lot of dissolved oxygen
B: boron
BSA: Biological surface area
Ca: Calcium
Cl: Chloride
Cu: Copper
DC: Direct current, mostly 12 volts supplied by a battery or inverter
DFT: Deep flow technique
DIY: do it yourself
DLI: Daily light integral
DO: dissolved oxygen
DWC: deep water culture
EC: Electrical conductivity
FCR: Feed conversion rate
Fe: Iron
GH: water hardness
GPH: Gallons per hour
HD: high density
IBC: Intermediate bulk container
K: potassium
KG: Alkalinity
Kwh: Kilowatts hour refers to the amount of kilowatts drawn in one hour.
LD: low density
LED: Light-emitting diode
MBBR: Moving bed biofilm reactor
Mg: magnesium
Min: mineralization tank

Mn: Manganese

Mo: molybdenum

N: nitrogen

NFT: nutrient film technique

NH3: toxic ammonia

NH4: less toxic ammonium

Nitrobacter: bacteria that convert nitrites to nitrates

Nitrosomonas: bacteria that convert ammonia to nitrites

NO2: nitrite

NO3: nitrate

OMRI: organic materials review institute

P: phosphorus

PEX: cross-linked polyethylene used for plastic piping

pH: a scale used to specify how acid or basic water is. The lower, the more acidic. Pure water has a pH of 7.

PPF: photosynthetic photon flux

PPFD: photosynthetic photon flux in a certain area

ppm: parts per million

PVC: polyvinyl chloride

Rafts: styrofoam insulation panels that float on the water in a deep-water culture system.

RAS: recirculating aquaculture systems

S: sulfur

SIP: self-irrigating plant bed

SLO: Solids lifting overflow

SSA: specific surface area. This refers to the total surface area of a material per cubic feet.

T5: Length of a specific fluorescent light tube

TAN: total ammonia nitrogen

UVI system: University of the Virgin Islands system. The most talked-about commercial aquaponics operation.

Zn: Zinc

Conversions

Temperature

Celcius (°C)	Fahrenheit (°F)
0	32
5	41
10	50
15	59
20	68
25	77
30	86
35	95
40	104

Volume
1 liter = 0.26 gallon (divide by 3.785)
1 gallon = 3.78 liter (multiply by 3.785)

$1ft^3$ = 0.028 $meter^3$ (divide by 35.315)
$1m^3$ = 35.31 $feet^3$ (multiply by 35.315)

Weight
1 gram = 0.035 ounces (divide by 28.35)
1 ounce = 28.35 grams (multiply by 28.35)

Length
1 foot = 0.3 meter (divide by 3.281)
1 meter = 3.28 feet (multiply by 3.281)

Area
1 $foot^2$ = 0.093 $meter^2$ (divide by 10.764)
1 $meter^2$ = 10.76 $feet^2$ (multiply by 10.764)